ALMOST COPING

TERRY AUCHTER

Illustrated by Christa Howe

PHUNN PUBLISHERS WILD ROSE, WISCONSIN 54984

ALMOST COPING

Published by Phunn Publishers
Wild Rose, Wisconsin 54984

Library of Congress Catalog Card Number: 83-61876
ISBN: 0-931762-20-0

Printed in U.S.A.

ALMOST COPING

by Terri Auchter

"A SLICE OF LIFE COMMENTARY ON THE FEELINGS AND EMOTIONS THAT AFFECT EACH AND EVERY ONE OF US."

—Don Kosterman
Badger Features Syndication

"BETWEEN HEARTY LAUGHS AND A LUMP IN MY THROAT, I IDENTIFIED WITH EVERY WORD."

—Niki Adam-Casimiro
Editor and Writer

"IF YOU'VE EVER HAD A FAMILY, YOU'LL LOVE TERRI AUCHTER'S BOOK!"

—Patricia Evans
Mother of Six

"TERRI AUCHTER WRITES WITH SUBTLE APPRECIATION FOR THE HUMOROUS ELEMENT WHICH TURNS UP ALMOST EVERYWHERE IN LIFE. SHE MAKES US LAUGH IN SPITE OF OUR FLAWS, OR, RATHER, BECAUSE OF THEM."

—Gareth Wilson
Family Counselor

To my children, Maryann, Rick, Judy and Ellen,
and my husband, Dick,
and to every mother who has ever
felt like running away from home
but couldn't find her car keys, so
she baked a batch of chocolate chip
cookies instead.

CONTENTS

A Happy New "Me" Year

The trouble with making New Year's resolutions is that I have never been able to keep them.

I have always been too hard on myself—resolving to eat less, to exercise more, to never buy anything just because it is on sale, and to floss my teeth three times a day.

No wonder I couldn't keep them. But this year is going to be different. I should have no trouble keeping these resolutions. I'm going to accept me as I am.

I resolve never to feel guilty about what I eat. If I have one of my famous Dieter's Sundaes—a heaping tablespoon of ice cream with chocolate syrup, eaten from the spoon over the kitchen sink—I will enjoy it. If my hips are padded, so what. Flesh helps to keep me warm during cold winter evenings.

I'm not athletic. I'm clumsy. My best sport is reading. Nobody ever dislocated any major part of her anatomy while reading a book. It's a safe sport and I enjoy it. So I vow not to feel guilty because I don't jog or play tennis. For years I have apologized for this—even lied. I have claimed to be suffering from jogger's elbow or tennis knee (or is it the other way around?) Never again!

I will not feel guilty when I lose my temper and scream. I've always felt bad about losing control. Then I read about Primal Scream Therapy where people have to pay money to learn to do what I've been doing naturally for years. I will continue to yell at times, but I will feel happy that it's not costing me a cent.

I will not hate myself because I impulsively bought a bright purple blouse on sale for $10.99 and will probably never wear it. It made me happy. It cost less than an hour of therapy and was not immoral, illegal, or fattening.

And I resolve never to feel guilty about saying "no." It's a lovely little word and it can keep me out of a lot of trouble. I will practice saying it in front of the mirror. And when I'm asked to do something I don't have time to do or do not care to do, I will let it roll easily off my lips.

Yes, I think this year I can keep all my New Year's resolutions. Now I think I will have a "tablespoon sundae." I may even use a dish.

HONEYMOON MYSTIQUE

Now that so many couples are living together before marriage, I think the mystique must be missing from the wedding night. A honeymoon can't hold many surprises for them.

Too bad. My wedding night was full of surprises. Especially for him.

We really didn't know much about each other when we first married. No wonder whenever we heard Frank Sinatra singing *Strangers in the Night* we said they were playing our song.

The first surprise for him was the fact that I wore make-up.

"What's this?" he asked, holding up my twenty-pound cosmetic bag.

"Oh, that. Just a little lipstick."

"There's more than lipstick in here."

"Well, maybe some eye shadow."

"Eye shadow? I didn't know you wore any."

"You thought I was born with blue eyelids? That's cute."

"And this? Looks like a medieval instrument of torture."

"Silly. That's my eyelash curler."

"You curl your eyelashes?"

"Oh, just once a day or so."

"What else do you have in your bag of tricks?"

"I don't consider this my bag of tricks," I said huffily. "Just a little help where nature needs to be improved upon."

"And what are all these rollers for? You don't mean —you can't mean—."

"That's right. You've married someone who doesn't have naturally curly locks. Want an annulment?"

He said, "No," but it was close. Couples today just don't know what they're missing.

The honeymoon trip was great for getting acquainted. I found out he squeezes the toothpaste from the bottom of the tube, is a morning person, and is always in a hurry.

He learned that I squeeze the toothpaste from the middle, am a night person, and like to move slowly, if at all.

Yes, a honeymoon is fun. It gave us the opportunity to find out for the first time just how incompatible we really are. But the fact that we have nothing in common seems to be just what we have in common. I wonder how many young couples can boast of that today.

I hate to sound smug, but that just may be the key to a successful marriage. Since we were incompatible at the start, we didn't have to waste a lot of time getting that way.

Could You Use His Toothbrush?

I remember my mother's favorite maxim regarding true love: "Could you use his toothbrush?" If I had listened to her, I never would have married. Using another person's toothbrush never has held great appeal for me.

But she didn't say a word about the pitfalls involved when a night person marries a morning person. Why didn't she warn me that marrying a man, who wakes up early *without an alarm clock* and who goes to bed at 10:00 p.m., was bound to put a strain on matrimonial bliss?

Oh, I do like mornings. I like them starting at 10:00 a.m. Of course, with children I have to get up early, but that doesn't mean I have to *wake up* early. There's a difference.

I find I can get up at 6:30 a.m., stagger off in the general direction of the kitchen, fix breakfast, drive the kids to school—and not remember any of it. In fact, I once drove them to the wrong school.

In order to ensure that I don't wake up, there is one sacred rule in our household. No one must expect me to speak, to ask or to answer questions at that hour of the morning.

On the other hand, You-know-who wakes up early and, to my utter horror, starts talking. He says things like

"Great day, isn't it?" "What do you think of that proposed tax cut?" and "Should we look around for a new car?"

Words, all strung together in sentences. Not a grunt or a moan or a yawn passes his lips.

When I get up, my mouth can never seem to work. The most I can get out is "mmmmmmmmm" or maybe "harrummph."

But by 10:00 p.m., my metamorphosis is complete. My eyes are bright, my tongue fully in gear, words and notions fill my head. I sparkle with effervescence.

He yawns.

I ask brightly, "What's on for tonight? The night is young, even if we're not."

He harrummphs.

I make witty remarks. ("Did you hear the one about the pilot who had trouble landing his plane because the runway was so short? After he finally got it down, he turned to his co-pilot and said, 'This runway sure was short, but was it ever wide!'")

He snores.

I've often wondered if we're still incompatible. But we're never awake at the same time long enough to find out.

"Isn't this a perfect morning for a 3 mile run?"

I KNOW WHO I AM

In this age of women's liberation, women are free at last to satisfy their needs, pursue their goals, seek meaningful relationships, and maintain their own identities. Finally I am free to be ME—if only I could figure out who ME is.

After fifteen years of marriage and four children, syllogistically it should follow that I am a housewife. However, can anyone really deserve the title of housewife who seriously considered selling her house to avoid cleaning it? Can someone, who finally throws the Thanksgiving turkey carcass out of the refrigerator only because she has to make room for the Easter ham, dare subscribe to *Good Housekeeping* or write "homemaker" as her occupation on credit card applications?

Therein lies the problem. Housewifery has been raised from a noble pastime to an occupation. Women's Lib has made it possible for a woman to be just as proud, whether she's a housewife or a nuclear physicist. But, by definition, occupation infers a certain dedication and singleness of purpose that I simply don't possess when it comes to the matter of home maintenance.

So, what's a woman to do? It seems to me that an alternate job description is needed—a term that could be used to describe someone like me who does not work outside the home, but doesn't really work *in* it either. This term could convey the same degree of involvement as the term "housewife", but denote an alternate lifestyle for a woman who believes it is more important to read six books in one week than to have six layers of wax on the kitchen floor. Such a term would alleviate any guilt the housework-hating woman might feel from being stuck with the label of housewife, a label she feels she neither deserves nor wants.

This type of woman is also one who is not home too much. She grabs any opportunity to get away from home, thus putting sufficient distance between her house and herself so she will not have to clean it.

For example, I will cheerfully donate my blood because it is so much more fun than vacuuming. I look forward to going to the dentist for the same reason. A really fun day for me was shepherding 25 first-graders on a tour of a chicken farm. My house really looked neat and tidy after spending all afternoon in a gigantic chicken coop.

In fact, it was just after that outing that I came up with the term for a woman like me. I have decided I am a "homesome."

"Homesome" has a nice homey ring to it, is not hard to spell, and yet does not mean the same as housewife. A homesome is someone who is home some of the time, and when she is home she is doing as little housework as possible.

This new term will not only solve my identity problem; it would make it easier for organizations which are looking for volunteers. For example, if the school needed help with the bake sale, they would check their records and only call on the homemakers and housewives for a contribution of homemade goodies. On the other hand, if they needed someone to spend a week or so painting the gym, they would call on the homesomes, knowing this group of women would be more than willing to help, for in so doing they would be unable to spend the time cleaning house.

Children would be aided by this new terminology, too. If a group wanted to play a quiet game of Monopoly and munch homemade cookies in spotless surroundings, they would go to the home of a friend whose mother is a housewife. However, if they had a fondness for oreos, and wanted to build a maze for their fourteen hamsters, they would head for the home of a homesome, confident that neither they nor the hamsters would be noticed in the clutter of a homesome's house.

I believe the use of this new terminology could be the answer to many women's identity crises. I am so thrilled with my new title that I thought of a motto to go with it:

"A home is not a home without a homesome."

List Making and Note Taking

You can divide the population of the entire country into people who make lists and those who don't.

I make lists. If I don't write it down, I'll never do it. There's a good chance I won't do it anyway, but at least if I've written it down, I might.

I also write notes to myself on the calendar. My whole life is chronicled by those little squares. I found an old calendar the other day. One note for May 1970 read "*Have the baby.*"

That's certainly succinct. But other times I can't decipher the meaning of what I've written. For example, under every Tuesday in June, I have written "*Drive Art—2 o'clock.*" Is Art someone I know? Drive him where? Finally I figure it out. It's not *Art* (capital A). It's *art* as in art lessons. My carpool day is Tuesday.

Under Wednesday I find "*Call vacuum.*" That's an easy one. Call and see if the vacuum is fixed. Since I'm in no hurry to have the vacuum back, I can skip this note.

Another one reads "*Patty will drive.*" That one still has me stumped. Obviously Patty will drive, but will she drive me or one of the children? And where am I or they going? I'll just have to wait until Wednesday and ask Patty.

The notes which really panic me are the kind where just a time is listed: "*Friday, 6:30 p.m.*" Am I having a dinner party? If so, I better call about the vacuum. Am I going to a dinner? Surely it will come to me before Friday. I hope.

Sometimes I get tough with myself and write notes of a more personal nature. I found one in the refrigerator this morning which read, "*You are fat! Do not eat anything in this fridge today!*" These notes always seem like a good idea when I write them, but they never do much good when I find them. I always figure I shouldn't take an anonymous note seriously, anyway.

My mother-in-law is a champion list-maker and note-taker. She has notes on every turkey served at every family Thanksgiving dinner going back for twenty-five years. She has terse notations about who was there, the size of the bird, was it tender, dry, too big or too small. She found me reading them one day and said, "I bet you think I'm crazy."

"Well, maybe a little crazy," I said. "Not one of those notes says, '*Don't you dare eat two helpings of anything, Miss Piggy.*' That's what I always put on my turkey notes."

To Emma

Let me introduce you to Emma. She was born of German ancestry more than seventy-five years ago, and was raised in Milwaukee. Her mother was a talented seamstress and her father was a cabinetmaker. She had one sister.

Those were the days when, if you spotted a penny on the sidewalk, you not only picked it up — you considered it your lucky day! Those, too, were the days when nothing was disposable. Everything was saved and used again. The twine the butcher used to tie up brown packages of liverwurst was saved and rinsed and used to truss up pigs-in-a-blanket for Sunday dinner.

Flour sacks were made into aprons and little girls' play dresses, and sheets were darned and later made into pillowcases when the worn spots got too big to be sutured with a darning needle. Mattresses were turned and aired often to prolong their life; rugs were beaten; and new clothes were soaked in salt water before they were washed, to keep them from shrinking.

Emma learned all these lessons in frugality and continued to practice them after she married and moved to another city.

She raised four children; her husband became very successful and the family prospered. She no longer had to save the twine and darn the sheets. But she did. Old lessons, learned young, stay with you.

Her children married and Emma became my mother-in-law. She watched silently as I used paper towels instead of rags for cleaning, as I used a dryer instead of a clothesline, and fed the children instant oatmeal. I never used a darning needle. She learned to put disposable diapers on my babies.

She viewed my new dishwasher skeptically, but said it looked like a nice gadget. However, when she stayed at our house, she did the dishes by hand. She even bought some of the new timesavers that twentieth century technology provided: a washer, a dryer, a mangle. And she bought plastic baggies. She also washed and dried them and stored them away for next time.

But whenever she saw me take something out of a baggie and toss the wrap in the trash, she never said a word.

As my own family grew, Emma lovingly watched their progress. If she thought having a calculator in grade school, or a ten-speed bike in junior high, or your own phone for your sixteenth birthday was not what she would have done for her own children, she never said so.

With her German sense of neatness and order, her house always glistened in bright scrubbed cleanness —deep-down, every corner, squeaky cleanness. It still does. But when she sat on the sofa in our house and her hands came across a stale donut under the cushions, other than expressing a ladylike "Oh, dear," she never said a word.

When I invited Emma and her bridge club over for a luncheon on what turned out to be a particularly harrowing day, and I used a new sheet for a tablecloth because I hadn't found time to iron the damask one, she not only didn't criticize—she admired my ingenuity.

During the early years of my marriage, when I was trying to cope with babies and schedules and carpools and housework and never seemed to quite catch up, Emma never criticized a single thing. When I burst into a hearty soliloquy extolling feminism and praising the progress of women's activism and liberation, she listened attentively. Looking back, I'm sure at times her tongue must have been bleeding as a result of her biting it.

This thoughtful, genteel lady never once gave me any advice. About anything. Not once.

I'm not a mother-in-law yet. But already I see my older children, who are away at college, sometimes doing things I wish they wouldn't do, or just doing things differently from the way I would do them. It's hard not to believe my own way is best. But more than once I've stopped myself from giving them unasked-for advice.

When this happens, I think of Emma. If I am a mother-in-law some day, maybe I will hold my tongue. At least I'm going to try. And Emma, I have you to thank for that. You'll be a hard act to follow, but I'm grateful to have had you for a role-model.

In fact, next time we're doing dishes at your house and you start washing the baggies, I'll dry.

No, I'm Not His Grandmother!

A new trend in society has women postponing motherhood for years or even decades.

No longer do we see women marrying and having babies while young, like we used to. Now motherhood is delayed in favor of a career.

I think it's great, but it might cause some real changes in our society.

Instead of baby showers, we'll probably be giving a little something toward the couple's IRA account.

Madison Avenue will have to scrap those commercials that make you guess which is mom and which is daughter. Where's the challenge if one is in support stockings, has grey hair, and wears a hearing aid?

Imagine a woman having her first child at thirty-eight, after her career and his are firmly established. I thought being a Girl Scout leader was trying enough without having to cope with hot flashes at the same time.

The manner in which people marry would change too. Weddings might have to be paid out of Social Security benefits. This could do a lot to bring back small weddings, especially if they are held on the front lawn of the Retirement Home.

Senior Citizen's seminars could offer courses in how to budget for your child's graduate school while living on a pension. PTA meetings would have informative talks like "Sex After Sixty" or "How to Repair Your Pacemaker."

Our society, which now venerates youth with such slogans as "*Don't trust anyone over thirty,*" will instead foster a respect for elders: "*Anyone under thirty is too young to be trusted.*"

It will also keep me from becoming a grandmother while still young enough to not look the part. Unfortunately, I'll never hear the words that so pleased my mother: "You, a grandmother? I would never have believed it."

One problem solved by delaying motherhood is obvious. No one will have to wonder what to do during retirement.

"It's Butter When It's Warmer"

Dear Mother Nature,

As I sit gazing at the frozen tundra, I have decided you should spend less time making margarine commercials and more time improving the weather.

It's so cold out today there's nothing 'motherly' about you. I could even swear you are a man.

"How cold is it?" you ask.

It is so cold that the weatherman didn't have nerve enough to tell us the wind chill factor.

It is so cold that the dog is eyeing the cat's litter box with envy.

It is so cold that, by the time I have put on my three pairs of socks, four sweaters, two scarves, a vest, a coat, and my husband's old army greatcoat, I don't fit behind the steering wheel of the car. So even if I could get it started, I couldn't go anywhere.

It is so cold that my children wore hats and mittens to walk to the bus, without my telling them. If you know anything at all about children, you know that's COLD!

It is so cold that I called my old friend in California so she could describe sunny, warm air to me over the phone. Yes, sunny, warm air—how it feels on your face, your feet—because I've forgotten what it's like to be warm.

It is so cold the snow is frozen.

It is so cold that, whenever I'm bored, I can watch the smoke from the neighbor's furnace blow out the chimney and hang there.

It is so cold that the tap water hurts my teeth.

My husband says it's colder than a... well, never mind what he says. Just take my word for it. And I certainly wouldn't fool Mother Nature.

What we need is a little high pressure system. Texas has plenty of 'em and you could send one our way. ARE YOU LISTENING, MOTHER?

Sincerely yours,

A frozen, barely likes it here anymore,
Wisconsinite

GREAT BICEPS ROCKING CRADLES

On a national talk show recently the subject was paternity leave — men who ask for time off from their jobs to care for their babies.

I don't think it will ever catch on.

One man said he used to be a stock broker, but now he would do anything to get out of the house. After three months of caring for a newborn and a toddler, he was ready to go out and dig ditches.

Another man said he had no idea staying home and caring for small children was such hard work. The stock-broker-turned-ditch-digger agreed wholeheartedly. "Ditch digging," he said, "is a real vacation compared to being a househusband."

Another man said his wife used to tell him about her day but he really couldn't comprehend it — and most of the time he really didn't listen to her anyway.

Aha! I think that's the crux of the problem!

When a husband has been away working all day, it's hard to explain that the baby has more gas than the Chevron station, that the two-year-old has learned to scale the kitchen cabinets and spent the day walking on the counter, opening cupboards and dumping sugar and coffee all over the floor, that the four-year-old has used Magic Marker to decorate his room although you were positive he was past that stage, and the six-year-old was sent home from school with stomach flu and you know how that goes through the family.

No, some things can't be explained. You just have to be there.

The sad part is that men on paternity leave can always escape by digging ditches. For a woman it's not that easy. Unless a woman has great biceps and loves shoveling, they'd probably hire a man anyway.

But at least some men are learning what women have known for a long time: the hand that rocks the cradle is attached to a body that is plumb tuckered out.

WHAT IS A FATHER?

What is a father?

A father is someone who will pick you up and carry you when your legs get really tired.

A father is someone who calls you his big man, even though you know you're little.

A father will sometimes bandage your cut finger with Scotch tape because he can't find the Band-aids.

A father will let you play out in the snow for a long time and not notice your hat fell off and your mittens are lost.

A father is someone who doesn't mind putting the worm on your fishing hook.

A father is someone who yells at you to get your bike out of the driveway.

A father will fix your bike, even though there's a football game on TV.

A father is someone who'll push you really high in the swing, so high you sometimes feel like you're flying.

A father will teach you to tie a knot that won't slip out.

A father won't scream if you put your hamster in his chair.

A father is someone who likes to read the newspaper in peace and quiet.

A father loans you money when nobody else will.

A father is someone who fixes great dinners like pizza and Kentucky Fried Chicken when Mom is sick.

A father will play ball with you even on Father's Day.

A father will roar with laughter whenever you tell him a "knock-knock" joke, even though he's probably heard it before.

A father will let you eat a hot dog at the ball game without washing your hands first.

A father will come to the Father-Daughter Breakfast, even though it's the opening day of trout season.

What is a father? My Dad. That's what. 

ARMCHAIR SHOPPER

There are some people who can walk into a store, buy a chair or sofa, and leave. No research, no comparison shopping. They just buy.

My husband is not one of those. He's been looking for a new chair to replace his favorite for more than a year, and he's not even close to making a decision yet.

This guy is normally decisive, confident, and aggressive. But when it comes to buying anything for the house, he's as lost as I am in a hardware store.

When we needed new carpeting, he researched it for weeks. We learned all about thread count per square inch of nylon versus acrylic fibers. We made so many trips to one carpet store that I finally invited the salesman over for dinner. We still exchange Christmas cards.

But buying a new chair takes even more time. He has sat down in every chair in every store from Green Bay to Milwaukee, and none will do.

It's either too high or too low, too soft or too hard, too roomy or too snug. I believe it's referred to in psychological terms as the "Goldilocks syndrome."

The chair he calls "his chair" is eighteen years old. It has been recovered twice. It's well broken in. In fact, it's broken. The arms wobble, the seat sags, and the springs poke him. After sitting in that chair, a friend from California said it made her homesick. It was like being in a minor earthquake.

I tell him he's not going to find a new chair just like the old one. It takes years of sitting to mold your chair to precisely the shape of your posterior.

But the great chair search continues. He's just invited me on a little trip to Chicago to look for a chair. If he doesn't find one there, I have a great idea. Maybe he could look for a chair in Florida or the Bahamas.

And I hear Mexico City is having a huge furniture clearance sale. I think we should check it out. After all, I don't want him to rush into buying anything, expecially since 'looking' can be so much fun.

CAT-PITULATION

When we first asked Big Daddy for a kitten, he said a lot of unprintable things and ended by screaming, "Over my dead body!"

I didn't take that as an unequivocal "no." So now we have a tiny ball of fur, called Poppy.

On her first day at our house, we are all waiting nervously for Daddy to come home from work. We decide to bribe him. We bake chocolate chip cookies, fix his favorite dinner, and I have a long cool drink waiting for him.

Tiny precious Poppy is adorably asleep in a wicker basket with a big satin bow.

Daddy walks in the door and Poppy jumps out of her basket and scales his leg.

Daddy says lots of things.

I say, "How about a cookie?"

He says, "How about an explanation? How can you do this to me when you know I hate cats!"

I say, "She's not a cat. She's a kitty."

He says, "She will grow into a cat."

I say, "You like squirrels. Couldn't you just pretend she's a squirrel?"

He says I have just reached a new low as a wife.

I say, "Why not sit down and have this nice drink?"

He does.

Poppy jumps up onto the table and knocks over his drink.

I shove another chocolate chip cookie into his mouth.

He picks up the kitten and deposits her across the room.

She comes back and purrs loudly as she rubs against his leg.

"You're a slow learner," he says to kitty.

I breathe a sigh of relief. At least he's talking to her. I wonder how many weeks before he starts talking to me again.

"Dad, remember when you said the only way we could ever have a kitty would be over your dead body? You were just kidding, right?"

HEART TO HEART

Although Valentine's Day is reported to have a long-ago beginning, I've heard it was Mr. Hall A. Mark who conceived the idea of this day as a nice way to sell a few penny cards and make people feel happy and loved at the same time.

It got out of control. I know it's out of control because I just saw a valentine that said "To My Favorite Babysitter" which cost $1.25. Give Americans a small holiday and they'll manage to turn it into something big.

When our children were little, getting ready for Valentine's Day always presented its own problems.

Have you ever tried to explain to a pre-schooler that the card he wants to give Grandma says, "To My Favorite Teacher"?

Or watched as a small child proudly showed you his valentines, finished at last, with his own name printed on the *outside* of every sealed envelope, and the recipients' names printed on all the cards *inside?*

Or argued with a child that he has to give valentines to the girls in his class too—while he responds that all the cards are "too mushy" to be given to any girl?

Or had to comfort a crying kindergartner because she didn't get as many valentines as her best friend?

Or tried to explain to a small one that the pretty card with all the paper lace costs a dollar more than she has in her little pocketbook?

But there's the happier side to Valentine's Day, too. A crayoned card, shyly given, reads "Happy Valentine's Day, Mommy." And a big "I love you," made out of construction paper, is pasted on the fridge.

One year there was a single rose which everyone chipped in to buy from their small allowances.

I remember the happy face of a child who found a red candy heart in her valentine from the boy who sat behind her in school and pulled her hair.

And who could forget the chubby hands delightedly ripping open a card that came in the mail addressed to him just like he was a grown-up!

Valentine's Day is a little bright spot in the middle of the darkest winter. If valentines still sold for a penny, it would be perfect.

FROM BAD TO VERSE

I was shopping for an anniversary card for Aunt Lilibeth and Uncle Harry. The new greeting card trend toward glossy photographs of people you don't even know presented quite a problem. I couldn't find one that even remotely resembled them.

The cards all showed beautiful sun and sand scenes with gorgeous lithe young people running gracefully as gazelles across the dunes. "Happy Anniversary to a Special Couple," the cards proclaimed.

Well, Aunt Lilibeth weighs in at around two hundred fifty pounds, and Uncle Harry is five feet, five inches tall. Neither of them has ever walked gracefully across sand dunes, much less run. And it's their thirty-fifth anniversary, and I know if Lilibeth got an eyeful of the gal on the front of this card, she wouldn't even let Harry see it.

But at least these cards say "Happy Anniversary." I found a lot of the new cards are just a picture with a blank page on the inside. Now, if I wanted to write a letter, I would; but what I'm here for is a card, not a blank page where I have to fill in my own sentiments. Hallmark, I'm paying you 95 cents to think for me. The least you can do is provide a verse.

Of course, there is an abundance of comic strip characters to choose from: Charlie Brown, Snoopy, and the whole Peanuts gang, Ziggy, and the irrepressible Muppets. It's hard to find a card with a simple sprig of daisies on the front — unless Kermit the Frog is holding the bouquet.

The contemporary cards offer another dilemma. Some of them are x-rated and some are a little too familiar. I picked up one which was intended for a sister in a religious order: "There's nun greater than you. Happy birthday."

Finally I found the perfect card for Aunt Lilibeth and Uncle Harry. It, too, showed a lady frolicking on the sand dunes, but it won't raise Harry's blood pressure.

Thank you, Miss Piggy, for being there when I really needed you. ❀

Blah Humbug

Everybody I know is sleepy. A friend of mine even said the only decision she made all week was whether to take a nap or to lie down and read a book. I know the only exercise I've been getting lately is yawning.

What is this strange phenomenon that seems to come every year right on the tail of the January thaw? It's the "February blahs" and the symptoms are easy to spot.

If you sit and stare a lot until even staring becomes such a chore that you give up and shut your eyes, you're a victim of the February blahs.

If the phone rings and you can't manage to answer it in ten rings, even though it's only four feet away, you've got 'em.

If you throw a load of laundry into the machine but have to take a nap in order to muster enough energy to put the clothes in the dryer, you're a victim of February.

If your husband comes home and asks what you did today and you snap, "I got up, didn't I!" — well, join the group of blahful souls.

What's a person to do? One great solution is to take off for sunny climes and tropical beaches and just sleep on the beach until March. Hawaii would do nicely. Unfortunately, most of us can't swing that. Of course we could just sleep at home until March; but small children, big children, husbands, and society in general frown on that.

We could form a "Committee of Blah-ers" to study the problem. By the time the committee's task force was formed, it would be March.

Or you can do what I do—tackle some monumental chore around the house that holds your interest. One February I spent the entire month scraping all the waxy yellow build-up off the floors with a steak knife. Another time I got pregnant. As a matter of fact, I think I did that several times in February. I don't really recommend that as a solution to the blahs. It does give you something else to think about, but then you're stuck with this solution for at least the next eighteen years.

One fine February I took up oil painting. That year the blahs lasted for an extra month. Whenever I looked at my masterpieces, I had a relapse.

I spent another February spraying plastic flowers with gold metallic paint. Then I sprayed the vases they were in. I branched out and sprayed the tables, the headboards, bookcases, and knick-knacks. Thank heaven March rolled around just as I was aiming at the dining room table.

I guess there's really no simple solution for the you-know-whats. Now, if someone will hand me that mosaic tile kit, I'll try to have this wall mural of Mt. Rushmore finished by the Ides of March.

Ballast, Balance and Boots

I'm glad spring has just about sprung. Except for a stray blizzard here and there, I can quit wearing my boots to cocktail parties.

I think boots are what I really hate about winter. There are some people who can navigate just fine on ice and snow in four-inch heels, but I'm not one of them.

Being balanced has never been one of my strong suits, and I don't stand up too well, either. I think I was born with just a tiny bit too much ballast on one side of my brain, which is great for writing humor but not so handy for walking on slippery pavements.

I've always had the problem, but it seems to be worse since I broke my leg. (I broke it, by the way, by falling over when I was just standing still on cross country skis. Anything you may have heard about my breaking it during the giant slalom competition at Aspen was slightly exaggerated.)

Now I have to wear boots at all times in winter — not the sleek fashion type with high heels, but the clumpy chunky kind with two-inch tire treads for soles.

Even then, I make slow progress on foot. I once took so long crossing an icy parking lot to a restaurant that, by the time I made it inside, my friends were already ordering dessert.

It can really be embarrassing. While visiting my son at college after an ice storm, he said I was walking so strangely his roommates would wonder whose granny was visiting.

My slow mincing gait also inspires derision from my peers. "That walk...oh, yes...Frankenstein in that horror movie..."

Yes, I'm glad the snow is on its way out so I won't have to clomp along in boots anymore. I will wear my summery sandals with the high heels and the delicate straps. And the way this winter has been, that should be around June first!

THE STARS DON'T KNOW IT ALL

Horoscopes are a great diversion and make for fun reading. Sometimes, however, an interpreter is needed to really figure them out. So I've compiled a *Guide to the Translation and Better Understanding of Horoscopes.*

HOROSCOPE: You will meet someone who sparks your innermost flame of desire.

TRANSLATION: The repairman will come to fix your furnace.

HOROSCOPE: You are asked to consider purchase, investment, or change that will alter domestic situation.

TRANSLATION: The kid wants a dog.

HOROSCOPE: Recent investment or business maneuver will pay surprise dividend.

TRANSLATION: You find a quarter while vacuuming the rug.

HOROSCOPE: An obstacle is transformed to steppingstone for progress.

TRANSLATION: You trip over the skateboard in the driveway, but manage to right yourself and get a wild ride to the trash cans.

HOROSCOPE: Focus on surroundings, home, domestic changes, possible purchases of property.

TRANSLATION: You go to a rummage sale.

HOROSCOPE: Wider recognition is due; superior recognizes your capabilities.

TRANSLATION: After only three days, the plumber comes to fix your sink and admits you've got a problem.

HOROSCOPE: Follow through on hunch. Intuitive intellect is honed to a razor sharpness.

TRANSLATION: You really shouldn't wash the windows today; it's going to rain.

HOROSCOPE: You bask in a glow of good feelings. Family member lends moral support.

TRANSLATION: *Your son tells you you're as pretty as the Incredible Hulk when he turns green.*

HOROSCOPE: Feeling of restriction could be mostly illusion; you have more room than might be anticipated.

TRANSLATION: *Those pantyhose, which are cutting off your circulation even though they promised one size would fit all, WILL stretch out.*

HOROSCOPE: Accent on possession, locating missing articles. Heed inner voice.

TRANSLATION: *So you misplaced your wedding ring. Freud didn't know everything.*

HOROSCOPE: Relatives, trips, close neighbors and phone calls dominate scenario.

TRANSLATION: *It's your week to carpool.*

HOROSCOPE: Ask questions, find out where you stand, especially with member of the opposite sex.

TRANSLATION: *What do you mean — you invited your mother to spend the summer so I wouldn't get bored?*

HOROSCOPE: Vitality makes a comeback; creative juices flow.

TRANSLATION: *Instead of watching Phil Donahue today, you switch to public broadcasting's lively offering: "Teach Yourself German."*

HOROSCOPE: You win friends and influence people; your position is stronger than might be imagined.

TRANSLATION: *Congratulations! You've just been named Girl Scout Cookie Chairman.*

HOROSCOPE: Power-play time. Timing, judgment are on target.

TRANSLATION: *You can turn that mattress all by your lonesome.*

HOROSCOPE: There are secrets to be revealed. You could be beneficiary.

TRANSLATION: *The rabbit died—again!*

SUN, MOON AND STARS

What is a mother?

A mother is someone who worries about you when you're sick, even though you're over thirty-five and have children of your own.

A mother is someone who always said, "No trouble, I love to bake cookies." And years later you learned she would rather spend a whole afternoon at the dentist than an hour in the kitchen.

A mother will not ask you whatever happened to Harold? when she knows you'd prefer to forget about it.

A mother will type your term paper because she says she doesn't have anything better to do on a Sunday afternoon.

A mother will put in a good word for you when a neighbor asks how you are at mowing lawns.

A mother is someone who somehow always forgets to turn off your bedroom light after you have had a bad dream.

A mother will sometimes yell like a banshee at you when she thinks you're doing something dangerous.

A mother has a lap big enough for both you and your baby brother.

A mother still hangs the Christmas ornament you made in kindergarten on the front of the tree.

A mother always reminds you to put your tooth under your pillow so the tooth fairy can come in the night.

A mother is a person who makes mistakes, loses her temper, sometimes makes a fool out of herself, and has her share of problems with wrinkles and bad habits,

A mother may work outside the home or in it — probably both. She may jog or play tennis or racquet ball. She may run a computer, be a pink lady, or practice medicine. She may be married or be a single parent.

A mother may be some or most of these, but she has something in common with every other mother. She loves you, warts and all.

Mother Dear, M.D.

For years the pediatrician's office was like my second home. I left a few of the children's cherished toys and my favorite Agatha Christie in the waiting room, so we always felt comfy.

I had practically a direct line to the office. "Hi, it's me again." They all knew who it was.

It all started when the first baby was two weeks old and got the hiccups. I tried all the cures listed by Dr. Spock, and then took her to our doctor. From that time on, I was hooked. I was always busy dragging babies to the doctor: babies who spit up all the time, babies who cried too much, babies who ate too much, and babies who just looked odd to me. I was their mother, so who was a better judge of their need for medical attention?

I think it was after about ten years of running a jitney service to the clinic that I realized I could handle a lot of this stuff myself.

For instance, if the child looked odd, well, he probably took after Uncle Harold who still looks odd. Or take beads stuck up noses. Our kids would find beads or little buttons from games and poke them up just far enough so you could see them but couldn't get them out. I'm sure it was some kind of quirk for which Freud would blame Mommy for feeding them spinach at too young an age.

Anyway, after years of running to the doctor with those beaded noses, I was without a car one time and discovered I could lay the child down on the kitchen counter, take a pair of tweezers and presto—goodby beads and buttons.

I also became adept at butterfly bandages and diagnosing possible fractures. (If you can't hobble as far as the refrigerator, x-rays are a good idea.)

The other day I ran into our pediatrician. He said he hadn't seen me for months and, since I used to be a member of the visit-your-doctor-daily club, he wondered what had become of me.

I told him I had learned to handle little medical emergencies myself. And if he ever wanted that mole removed from his chin, just to drop by any time. I'd take care of it for him.

✚ ✚ ✚

GRANDPARENTS KNOW HOW

Grandparents are nice for children to have for so many reasons.

Grandparents are never in a hurry.

"Grandpa always reads us really long bedtime stories and doesn't skip over any parts."

"When Grandma takes me for a walk, she walks real slow and lets me stop and smell all the flowers."

"When Grandpa takes me fishing, he never looks at his watch."

"Grandma likes to have me help her in the kitchen. She doesn't yell if the egg shells fall in the batter."

Grandparents always tell the truth, no matter what.

"Mother, Grandma told me your room was such a disaster when you were a kid that one day she shut the door and didn't open it again for seven years."

"Grandpa told me he caught you smoking a cigarette in the tool shed when you were in junior high."

"Grandma told me you didn't learn to ride a two-wheel bike until you were ten."

"Grandpa says he can tell I'm gonna be a great baseball player when I grow up."

"Grandma says I'm the prettiest girl in the world and will probly be a movie star someday."

Grandparents have a way of making any day a special day.

"Grandma says she made this dress for me because she didn't have anything special to do, and I can wear it right away — today."

"Grandpa made this bird house and gave it to me and it's not even Christmas."

"Grandma baked a three-layer cake for me and it isn't even my birthday."

"Grandpa told me to keep his old pocket watch because he doesn't have room for it in his desk anymore."

"Grandma let me dress up in her clothes and put on her face powder because she said I'm more fun to watch than TV."

"Grandpa pitched a tent in his backyard so I can go camping."

Grandparents know how to take some of the ache out of the heartache of growing up.

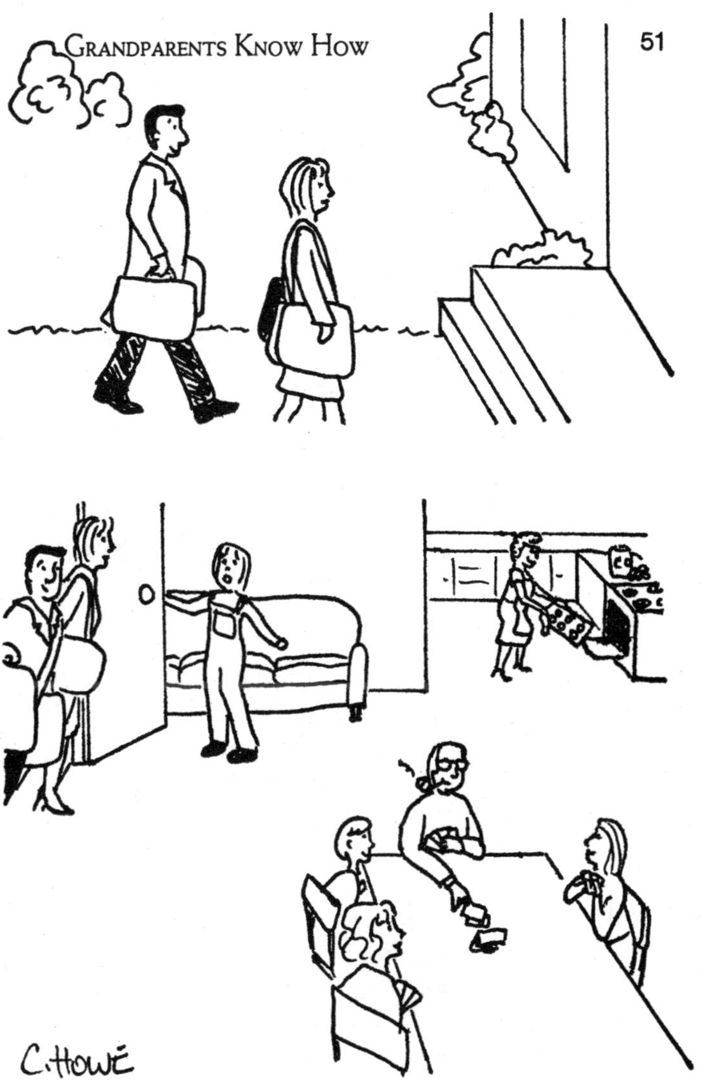

"Could you take a little longer vacation? We're still having fun with grandma and grandpa."

VOLLEYS OF DOLLIES

Over the years, I have probably bought more than my share of toys. I've often wondered how a child of two, who can't yet string more than two words together, can always manage to convey the message that she wants a battery-operated doll for her birthday.

One of my first experiences with such a doll was with a creature called Baby First Step. When its batteries worked—which was once on the day we bought it and again three years later when I was about to give it away—Baby First Step would take a few lumbering steps. Our daughter was three years old and certainly wanted that doll.

Her sister was one and just starting to walk. "Why do you want a battery-operated doll when you have the real thing?" I asked the older child. She looked at me, stamped her little foot and said, "Daddy will bring it on my birthday." I lost the argument.

Another doll, which I loathed, was Baby Alive. This one required six batteries and enough baby food to keep a real baby full for a week. This doll actually chewed, but what it did with all that food after it ate would not be pleasant to read about.

We also had Timey Tell, a doll with a big watch, who talked and said things like, "Three o'clock. Time for my nap." With four children of my own chattering away, I surely didn't need a fifth one telling me what to do.

When our last child was born, a friend asked me how the baby's room was decorated. I answered that it was done in "early GI Joe." The baby was sharing a room with her brother and that plastic soldier. Of course, GI Joe had a lot more stuff than the brother had.

GI Joe didn't need a battery, but he certainly needed his own closet. His outfits included fatigues, a diving suit, a space suit, and full-dress uniform. He also had to have a barracks to live in, a jeep to drive, and a replica of an Hawaiian village for R and R. He lived better than we did.

He often dated Barbie when Ken wasn't around. With Barbie's house, camper, car, beauty parlor and movie set, they took over at least two bedrooms and the dining room. Add to that Barbie's little sister and best friends, and Ken with his friends, and you have the real reason we had to sell a nice house and move to a bigger one.

We don't have dolls stumbling around and eating us out of house and home now. We've progressed to video games.

Before, when something went wrong, it was simple to buy new batteries. Now we have to call a TV repairman. I never thought I'd say this, but I think it was easier living with Barbie and Ken than with Pac Man and Space Invaders.

BETWIXT OR BE-TEEN

When does a child become a teenager?

I've seen it happen as young as eleven and as old as fifteen. I guess chronological age doesn't determine it as much as some inner clock saying it's time now to drive your parents crazy.

Overnight a perfectly happy, docile child can change into a hip, flippant you-know-what.

I've tucked a child in at night, put a teddy bear in her arms, and sighed with pleasure at her angelic countenance before I turned out the light.

The next morning she got up, announced she would suffer unspeakable anguish if she didn't get a phone of her own by nightfall, plugged herself into a curling iron, turned the stereo on high, and said nobody understood her at all. EVER!

The first time this happened, I thought it was temporary and would blow over in a day or two. It lasted seven years.

I'm no longer the innocent I was then. I've been through it three times already. Now when I tuck the youngest in at night, I look for telltale signs that the metamorphosis is about to occur. Is that a *Seventeen* magazine next to the Nancy Drew mystery on the bookcase? Is that lip gloss hidden under the skateboard? Is that a picture of Tom Selleck next to one of Miss Piggy on the bulletin board?

How long do I have before another daughter trades in her Girl Scout uniform for Calvin Kleins?

How long do I have before this one has a telephone plugged into one ear and a radio earphone plugged into the other? Before she tells me pizza is the only food she likes?

How long before what once made her happy, like trips to the zoo and to Grandma's house, will become boring and unendurable? When will her vocabulary be full of words like "crusty" and "grody" and "half-decent"?

She comes home from school and throws her books on the chair. She wanders over to the stereo. I stiffen, holding my breath, earplugs at the ready. She runs her hands over the speakers, then casually turns away. She turns on the TV, finds a Bugs Bunny cartoon, and happily flops into a chair.

I'm safe. For at least another day.

HYSTEREO

I've noticed that no self-respecting jean-clad teenager will get into a car unless its radio is blasting out rock. It's as if the car won't run on gas alone, but must have music to make its tires turn.

I've become hysterical about this phenomenon, ranted, raved, stamped my size nine army boots, and threatened to have the car radio disconnected. All without results.

Last week I rolled up in front of the high school. I had WVMS cooing a tune from my time, *Earth Angel.* They don't make 'em like that any more. I hummed along. *"EEEEEEEarrrth Annngelllll. . . ."*

I scanned the school yard and saw six girls headed my way. Each one wore a down-filled vest (blue), a sweater (navy blue), clean faded jeans, and hair blown dry to the height of fluffiness and shining with the sheen which comes from gallons of conditioner.

"Which of you is my daughter?" I asked.

One of the down-filled vests stepped forward. "Mom, it's me."

"Oh, yeah?" I said. "Prove it."

She flashed the monogram on her sweater.

"Okay," I said. "The initials match. Hop in."

"Not until you change the station on the radio," she replied. "I won't listen to that old-time music. It gives me a headache. How can you call that stuff music? Why not just listen to Larry Welk and be done with it?"

I was hurt. I may never see thirty-two again, or even thirty-seven, but I'm hip, I mean decent — or half-decent. I swing with *Earth Angel.*

I switched stations. John Denver sang to his love, Annie.

"Not that middle of the road," she hissed.

"What middle of the road? I'm in my lane."

"The station, Mother. The station is playing middle of the road music."

She switched it rapidly. Something called REO Speedwagon blared out what sounded like *"Time for Me to Fly."*

How true, I thought, *I really am ready to fly.*

She turned up the volume. Great waves of sound filled the car.

"TOO LOUD," I shouted. I felt like a Lilliputian trapped in a stereo with the lid down.

"WAY TOO LOUD!" I screamed. No one answered. Who could hear me over the din?

When I decided to become a mother, I always figured that someday I'd have fallen arches, stretch marks and cellulite. But nobody warned me that my hearing would be the first to go.

TEEN TIME WARP

Teenagers have an interesting concept of time. Actually, it starts long before adolescence. It just gets worse as they become teenagers.

For example, all my children have assumed that I have been around for an extremely long time. At the age of seven, Number One Daughter asked me if I had known Jesus— personally. Number One Son asked me if I had voted for Washington in his second presidential election. And they have all asked me, at one time or another, what my feelings were when Orville and Wilbur Wright took off.

As they grew older, their idea of time improved somewhat.

Our daughter would say, "Mom, there's an old silent movie on TV tonight. Want to watch it? It should bring back memories of you and Dad taking in a flick on Saturday night."

Putting me in the era of silent movies is an improvement over being the one who got out the vote for George.

However, as they pass through this stage and into teendom, their sense of time is still a trifle warped. The other day our seventeen-year-old son was making plans for Friday night.

"Where are you going?" I asked.

"I'm on my way to the school dance."

I should have known. He was wearing his running shoes, the pair with only six holes, and a shirt which carried the message: "I'm a Wild and Crazy Guy from Neenah, Wisconsin." Obviously, he had dressed with care.

"How late can I stay out?" he asked.

"How late do you think you should be able to stay out?" I asked bravely. (I had just read this book, *Talking to Your Teen as a Person,* and it said to respond to questions on rules in this manner.)

"How about until Sunday?" he replied.

"I have to do a report on the Civil War. What was it really like?"

"How about until 11 p.m. Friday?" I countered. I made a mental note to throw out the book.

But this same teen has a very precise sense of time regarding some aspects of his life.

He leaves cryptic messages for me like *"Pick me up from track practice at 3:56 p.m."* and *"Can you have dinner ready by 5:23 p.m.? I'm going to the game and Mike is picking me up at 5:47."*

Our daughter also has a time problem. She thinks nothing of leaving for school at 7:15 a.m., staying after school to watch a baseball game, and sauntering in at 6:30 p.m. One day she came home from school so late I was considering an ad to rent out her room. But this same child will call me for a ride home from school because the bus is running five minutes late and she simply cannot wait for it.

I tell her anyone who was old enough to vote for George Washington is too old and tired to come and pick her up.

VINTAGE VERNACULAR

My vocabulary is full of old-fashioned words which seem to confuse some people.

The other day I told my daughter's friend to put her books on the drainboard. She stood motionless for a long time. Finally she asked, "What's a drainboard?"

To me, the long kitchen counter that runs around my sink is a drainboard. That expression is older than I am, and I understand it came from the old wooden counters which had grooves in them for draining dishes. It's about the same vintage as the hitching post.

I say it because my mother said it, and her mother said it before her. And in that day and age it made sense.

I always refer to the refrigerator as the icebox. The beach house, where I spent summers as a child, had an icebox. It was a wooden cabinet with big shiny metal hinges. You had to put out a card for the iceman, marked for 10 or 15 or 25 pounds, so he would know how much ice to deliver. You could store ice cream in the icebox only on the days you had a fresh block of ice.

My grandfather always called the TV a radio, since for forty years he had a radio sitting where the TV was eventually placed, and he said it would always be a radio to him. It was a radio with pictures.

He also called most cars "roadsters." Motels were "motor courts," any department store was a "Sears

Roebuck," and a stove was a "fire," (as in "Did you put the chicken on the fire yet?")

Grandma always called a blouse a "waist" and a purse a "pocketbook." A sofa was a "settee."

The other day my daughter called from school to say she had forgotten her milk money and her lunch. She said, "I left the money on the drainboard and my lunch in the icebox."

It's nice to know there's someone carrying on the family tradition.

✠✠✠

THE FAMILY CONNECTION

It was a Sunday, and for a change everybody was home. I decided this phenomenon should not go unnoticed. To celebrate this unusual occurrence, we would all engage in something extremely rare at our house — conversation.

"Now, I want us all to talk — really communicate," I announced enthusiastically.

There was heavy silence.

"Well," I smiled sweetly, "who would like to start?"

"I will," answered ten-year-old Herman.

"Go ahead, Dear," I prompted.

"Is a joke OK?"

"A joke will be fine."

"Another one of his dumb jokes," moaned one of his siblings. "We'll all try to laugh."

"That's enough," I said through clenched teeth. "Let Herman tell his joke."

"It's one I just heard. See, there was this farmer and he had nine daughters, and this traveling salesman came by—."

"That's enough, Herman!" I interrupted.

"Whaddya mean that's enough? I just got started."

"Yeah, don't repress him, Mom," another sibling shouted. "This could lead to real problems later in life."

"Yeah, Mom, it's a great joke," Herman yelled.

"According to my psychology prof, a parent who constantly interrupts a child has a deep-seated need for—."

"Are we paying that big fat tuition to teach you to insult your mother?" hissed Big Daddy.

"It's a waste of money, all right. Why not send him to a work farm instead?" Lydia shouted. "A friend of mine—."

"What friend?" Herman asked. "She doesn't have no friends."

"ANY friends," I corrected.

"Right. See, even Mom knows you don't have no friends."

"Mooooootherrr, make him stop!"

There really is nothing like a real conversation. With a little luck, maybe it will be another six months before we're all home together again for a family talk. " "

DRIVING ME CRAZY

If anyone asks me why I have this nervous tic in my eye and why my head turns from side to side in a constant rhythm, my only explanation is that another of my children has his temporary driver's license.

I got the tic from shuddering. I've shuddered a lot since the first one to learn to drive suffered from a slight perception defect and drove so close to parked cars I could smell the leather of their upholstery. The constant head movement comes from checking intersections.

I wish I had the confidence these new drivers exude. I remember when Number One Son breezed in and asked if he could borrow the car.

"Where are you going?" I asked innocently.

"Florida."

"Florida!" I shrieked in my characteristic calm. "You've had your driver's license for one hour and you want to drive to Florida?"

"Of course. After all, Mom, one of my friends took off for California right from the Department of Motor Vehicles. The ink wasn't even dry on his license."

We compromised. I let him drive the dog to the vet.

I suffered the permanent tremors in my hands one sunny Sunday. I was sitting in the family room, which is behind the garage, when suddenly I felt the earth move. A religious experience? Was I being born again? Earthquake?

None of the above. It was Number One Daughter backing the car out and taking the garage with her. As I stared at the rubble of bricks and the listing garage, she waved gaily and said, "Don't worry, Mom. I'll be home by six."

Our third child just received her temporary license, and I took her on her first practice run.

"Mom, I don't think you have any confidence in my driving," she told me as we started off.

"Why do you say that?" I asked her.

"For one thing, I can't drive with your foot on the brake. And quit praying. We're still in the garage."

We zoomed down the street—*backward*.

"You've got it in reverse!" I shouted.

"I know that, Mom. I thought I'd practice backing up first. Then I'll practice a Y-turn. They always want you to do that when you take your test."

"How about just practicing driving down the street?" I suggested sweetly.

"Do they ask you to do that when you take the test?"

Luckily the blaring radio drowned out my reply.

Both my eyes have tics now. But I have made a decision. When our fourth child gets her temporary license, I plan to put both cars up for sale. If she wants to learn to drive, she'll have to make arrangements through Hertz first.

TOMMY

Recently I attended a sports banquet honoring the athletes at my son's high school.

It began, as most banquets do, with chicken and gravy and mashed potatoes. The large dining room was filled with football players, cross-country runners, soccer players, cheerleaders, baseball players, golfers, volleyball players, wrestlers, tennis players, coaches and parents. Three hundred and fifty of us.

After dinner, slightly logy from too much chicken, we settled back in our chairs and sipped our coffee, knowing we were in for a long but pleasant evening of speeches, award presentations, some not-too-funny jokes, and lots of clapping.

But one award changed all that. One award made this an evening of magic in which love seemed to fill the room, and everyone in it felt a special joy.

The award which changed everything was given to a young man named Tommy.

The football player who spoke of Tommy before giving him his award, told us Tommy had never missed a football practice or a football game. But this award was for much more than that.

Football practice starts in August, sometimes as early as 7:00 a.m. By noon it is hot, and running wind sprints is no fun. But Tommy is always there, shouting encouragement and telling every player, "I love ya—you can do it!"

Need something? Tommy will get it for you. Or the Coach wants something done? Tommy will do it, no questions asked. Whatever needs doing, Tommy is happy to help.

You're probably wondering what position Tommy plays on the team. Well, Tommy doesn't play football. Tommy is special. He is retarded and he loves football.

At the end of his speech, the football player called Tommy up to the stage. Tommy was awarded a football letter and a trophy. His broad smile filled the room.

"I love you, Tommy," said the football player. He gave him a bear hug. The big burly football player and the slight, special young man embraced while three hundred fifty people looked on and felt the warmth from the two of them.

There was a hush, and then waves and waves of applause washed over Tommy. There were tears, too.

Thanks, Tommy, for a very special evening.

MY SON, MY SON

It's graduation time again. It seems like just last year I had a child graduating from high school. As a matter of fact, I did.

Obviously, I'll never win the Planned Parenthood Mother-of-the-Year Award.

This year our son is graduating. He has a new suit, with a vest, for the occasion. He looks like a very young banker. It's a shock to see him without a Levi's label on his backside.

His first suit didn't have a vest. It was a soft blue blazer with short pants and gripper snaps to make changing his diaper easier.

He has new shoes, too. Brown leather. Gone are the running shoes with so many holes it was a mystery how they stayed on his feet. His first shoes were white with high tops and he always untied them as soon as I put them on.

He has his hair styled now. I remember his first haircut when he was shorn of his fat blonde curls. He screamed. I cried.

He has a new set of luggage which he needs for college out of state. His first piece of luggage was a duffel bag for a weekend of camping out with the Cub Scouts.

He has an electric typewriter. He will need that, too. His first attempts at writing were more colorful. My lipstick on the living room wall.

He has his own house key now and keys to our car. His first conveyance was a plastic fire truck that he sat on and scooted around the floor. It ran on toddler power. Sturdy little legs propelled it around the house and around the block.

I guess you could say he's a man now. I know he would.

He's eighteen. He can vote and drink and be registered for the draft. He's grown up. I know it, too.

But why, as I watch him receive his diploma, do I still see him on that little fire engine, scooting across the yard and never looking back?

IT'S ONLY THE FIRST DAY

Bicycles, tricycles and hot wheels crowd sidewalks and driveways. Their drivers are jockeying for position in some unknown race for space.

Most of these drivers are alone in their quest, riding in their own lonely race. It's the first day of summer and alliances have not yet been formed. The groups and trios and duos that will break up and re-form all summer, like a child's kaleidoscope, have not yet taken shape.

By midsummer the alliances will be molded and fashioned. Johnny will play with Sean and Mike but never with Carl. Carl will play with Sean but not with Mike. Lisa's clubhouse will be a happy place with two or five or even eight other girls within its cardboard walls, but never with three. But none of this has happened yet. It is the first day.

Mrs. Callahan has just planted her red petunias along the walk. The yellow marigolds are small, still sharing space with the tulips. Later the tulips will be gone and the marigolds will be big and lush and she will sometimes yell, "Kids! Watch your bikes round my flowers!"

And Mr Layton will have his hose out every afternoon hosing down his house, his driveway and his sidewalk. He doesn't have any flowers so he waters his house. And he'll sometimes call out, "Careful running on that pavement there. It's wet." And it will be all wet and glossy and almost magically clean around his house until the sun dries the area and turns it back into a cracked rough cement walkway.

But today is just the first day and Mr. Layton is just rocking in his porch swing and not hosing down anything yet.

The teenagers are dressed in jeans, not shorts. It's still not that hot. Not like some days to come when even light shorts will feel heavy as lead; and after you sit on the curb for a while your clothes will stick to your body. Then even your T-shirt feels as hot as that scratchy wool sweater your mom makes you wear to school when it's below zero.

The lawns are green and sweet right now, even without any sprinklers on. Later they will be brown in some spots and the stubble will scratch your bare feet like dull needles in a pine forest.

But today there is just bright sun, not hot enough to make you perspire, and children trying to find each other so they'll have partners through the great adventure called summer. Today there's a soft breeze and the look of spring still lingers here and there with a stray daffodil, a muddy spot of ground. There's no great heat yet to inspire summer languor, nor any humidity to sap your energy.

Not yet. It's just the first day.

MUSCLES, MOVE!

It's that time of year again.

Time to lay in the supplies of low-fat cottage cheese, plain yogurt and carrot sticks. When the only swim suit I look good in is my old maternity suit, I have to admit I've not only forfeited the battle of the bulge — I have lost the war.

And my friend Eleanor helps me to forge ahead in my crusade against fat, cellulite and flabby upper arms.

Eleanor is thin. She has to wear a belt to hold up her size six jeans. She has never known what it is to have thigh rub against thigh as she walks. She has never had to wear pull-on pants with an elasticized waist. The words "*Does it come in large?*" have never passed her lips. She thinks saddle bags are just something cowboys have.

The other day, as she was sipping her basic black coffee, she asked me if I would like to go shopping.

"Grocery shopping?" I asked her.

"No, Terri, not grocery shopping. You know, that's one of your problems. All you think about is food."

"That's not true, Eleanor," I protested as I polished off the last of the apple strudel. "Just last week I thought about enrolling in night school. But I couldn't decide between a seminar on 'Microwave Cooking and Its Impact on Modern Society' and a course on 'The Wok's Effect on Sino-American Relations.'"

"Terri, what you need is a program of exercise. Take your mind off food."

I promised I would try.

The next morning I mounted the exercycle. I pedaled until my muscles screamed with pain, the perspiration flowed, and every fiber of my being felt alive and in agony. I felt at one with all those great athletes who have also pushed their bodies beyond their current levels of endurance to reach new heights of fitness.

I checked the odometer. I had pedaled half a mile.

Maybe what I needed was a more structured program of exercise. I enrolled in Madame LaComp's Fitness Class.

Madame lined us all up and measured our wrists. Whipping out a chart, she announced she could tell from our wrist measurements just how much weight we had to lose. When it was my turn, well — let it suffice to say that I am not fat. It's just that my wrist should be twenty-two inches around.

After the funsy of measuring came the exercise. If you have never performed jumping jacks to the tune of *Rocky* at 8:05 in the morning, consider yourself lucky.

Not only did I jump when everyone else was jacking, but I noticed everyone was wearing leotards and tights, while I was clad in sweatshirt and antique Bermuda shorts. I didn't have time to dwell on this, as the group plunged into sit-ups and hip-rolls, while a nifty recording of *Won't You Come Home, Bill Bailey* blared in the background.

An hour later Madame helped me to my feet. She thinks in three or four years I'll be in great shape.

Maybe it would be easier to have my wrist made larger.

SUITABLE FOR CELLULITE

I love summer. Really. Except for one or two teeny things, I think I love summer more than any other season.

The first exception to an otherwise perfect time of year is the fact that the children are home all day long. And they seem to multiply. Where there was one ten-year-old, there now are five. Where there were three teenagers, there now are seventeen.

Have you seen that commercial on TV where a happy mother collects all the neighborhood kids at her house because she serves gallons of Kool Aid? Well, I have the neighborhood at my house, and I never serve Kool Aid. In fact, I try not to feed them anything by mouth. Why encourage them?

The second exception to this idyllic time of year is the problem of what to wear.

Summer is hot and even I am not sufficiently eccentric to wear my raincoat all summer. This is the time of year you are supposed to enhance your sartorial image by wearing shorts and sun dresses and bathing suits.

What I'm looking for this year is a bathing suit with sleeves and a skirt. (Yup, the diet was a bust.) And what I'm finding is either a bikini — that's out — or a maillot.

The maillot is a one-piece bathing suit made of soft, soft material. It conceals nothing. Every bulge, every sag, every clump of cellulite is clearly visible under the material. There's nowhere to hide.

I tried one on and the realism was so overwhelming I vowed never to eat or swim again. Swimming won.

But I'm sure I'm not alone. And I think some enterprising person could make a fortune by designing a swim suit with sleeves. After all, fatty upper arms, that swing gaily long after you've quit waving your arms, are a common figure imperfection. Add a built-in Spandex slimmer-shaper in the tummy area and a thigh camouflaging skirt, and this suit would sell like dietetic hot cakes at a Weight Watchers' convention.

Believe me, once this suit hits the marketplace, Cheryl Tiegs may find herself out of a job.

FIVE INTO TWO WON'T GO

We have two cars, five drivers, and another driver waiting in the wings of the garage. It doesn't require a math major or Jimmy the Greek to figure out the odds are 5-2 against having a car to drive.

I've learned the odds are usually stacked against the house management.

The other night we hoped to celebrate our anniversary with a night out. I dressed carefully with visions of a candlelight dinner dancing in my head—a dinner with real napkins, no ringing phone, no background discussion of who broke whose blow dryer, and no macaroni in the main course.

I hummed *"Tonight's the Night,"* while pouring perfume over my body. Spouse took my arm and we glided out to the garage.

My screams brought the neighbors running.

"No car!" I shrieked hysterically. "Nothing in the garage! How could they? How?"

We took a cab.

But that evening's catastrophe was of minor proportions compared with what happened two weeks later.

Number One Daughter had driven one car to the fast-food chain where she works after school. Spouse drove the second car to work. I needed a car to chauffeur Number Three Daughter to the dentist.

I solved this problem by sending Number One Son, via bike, to the fast food chain where he traded the bike for the car. He drove home and announced he needed the car for a track meet. We then proceeded—Number One Son, Number Three Daughter and I— to drive to Spouse's office. I took Spouse's car while Son took the other car.

Meanwhile, Number One Daughter was permitted to leave work early and found a bike in the stall where the car should have been. She reported the car stolen and rode home on the bike.

While this was going on, Spouse left the office for a meeting across town and found no car in his parking

C.HOWE
"I need the car for work in 10 minutes."
"Can you drive me to cheerleading practice?"
"Could you drop me at the library?"
"I need a ride to Holly's house."

stall. He reported the car stolen. The officers arrived at our house just as Number One Son and I pulled into the driveway simultaneously, each driving a "stolen" car.

I think there is a lesson to be learned here. Perhaps Confucious could have put it succinctly by saying: "Never take car from another's parking stall without leaving note."

A House Divided

It seems to me that, as vacationers, children can be divided into two groups: the active and the passive participants.

For the active type there is never a wasted moment. Summer is all too short. This child dashes from one activity to another with all the frenzy of a politician campaigning on the eve of election day.

He builds a forty-foot maze for his hamsters on the dining room table, stages a morality play with costumes, builds a high jump for his backyard olympics, and puts on a circus featuring every animal in the neighborhood. Mothers have been known to place ads in the paper, attempting to cope with this whirlwind by trying to rent him out for the summer.

The flip side of the hyper/super kid is the passive child who regards summer vacation as one long relaxing time to sit. His most ambitious plans for the summer include watching "Laverne and Shirley" reruns.

This type of child has put a new creativity into doing nothing. He crawls out of bed late—but not too late for his favorite TV game show or "Gilligan's Island" rerun. You'd think he was in a coma, except for trips to the kitchen for more food. The great outdoors does not beckon, friends are acceptable only if they drop in, and any physical activity is frowned upon.

Shouting, "Get out and do something, ANYTHING!" is risky. Because, if this type does get up and off the couch, it is probably to put the hammock outside and spend the rest of the summer there—in full view of all the neighbors.

Ours is a house divided—half active and half passive.

The other day I shrieked, "Can't you rest for one minute? And what are all those boards for? If I told you once, I told you a hundred times, we don't need an addition on the garage. Relax!"

Passive stretched out his legs and let out a sigh.

"Not you," I screeched. "Him!"

Active kept right on hammering.

HIGH GEAR/LOW GEAR

Do you know what it's like to travel thousands of miles by car with a man who thinks rest areas are only for changing flat tires? Have you ever jogged through the Smithsonian? Or gone on every ride in Disney World with enough time left for a running tour of the Busch Gardens?

I can answer "yes" to all of the above. I owe it all to a husband who believes vacations are fun as long as you don't waste time relaxing.

"Let's get the show on the road," he booms cheerfully at 5:30 a.m.

Personally, I think 5:30 a.m. is an ungodly hour for anything. I have only been up that early twice. Once was to have a baby, and the other time was New Year's Day in 1960 when I had stayed up all night.

I have passed on my loathing for the early morning hours to all four children. However, good sports that we are, we gamely stagger out to the station wagon, muttering unkind statements under our collective breath. One of us strides to the car whistling, *Oh, What a Beautiful Morning*. (Yeah, HIM!)

We whiz over freeways until noon.

"Pit Stop!" he yells.

This is my cue. He pulls up at the Golden Arches and slows to a near stop. I leap from the car, order lunch for everyone, grab the order and run to my appointed station on the corner. While I have been fetching the food, he has been gassing up the car. After all, there isn't a moment to lose. This is a vacation.

Each afternoon we are permitted one calisthenics stop.

"Everybody out for three quick laps around the wayside," he shouts gaily.

This is pleasant enough if we are near a wayside, but the practice often causes stares and even outright heckling as we go through our paces in the middle of Boston Common or in front of Bloomingdales in Manhattan.

Once at our destination, our sightseeing is done in high gear. Being a low gear person, I get left behind a lot. I spent an enjoyable afternoon soaking my feet in a reflecting pool in Washington, D.C. They finally found me after they had completed their tour of the U.S. Mint, The F.B.I., and all of Congress.

My idea of a fun vacation is spending a week at a motel, pool-side, doing nothing more energetic than watching the hair grow on my legs.

I think my dream vacation will be postponed for a while. The other night my husband announced we were all going to Cincinnati on Tuesday—for lunch.

COTTAGE CAMARADERIE

When you own a cottage, summer is just one long siege of packing and unpacking.

Around the end of July, you begin to feel like a member of a small circus, forever folding your tent and quietly stealing away. While you're home, you're packing up to leave, and while you're at the cottage, you're packing to come home.

At least, that's the way it used to be. However, as the years have gone by, I have learned to eliminate some of the more bothersome aspects of packing.

For example, I used to bake ahead for these weekends, neatly labeling items with *"These yummys are for the cottage."* Now all I do is grab a jar of peanut butter and a package of hot dogs and shout "Geronimo! Everybody get in the car! We are leaving for the cottage — NOW!"

Despite the packing, cottages are fun. There's that lovely lake outside. Of course, the water temperature is usually a mite chilly, which is why I always buy a blue bathing suit. It matches the color of my body when I get out of the water.

When you own a cottage, there is never a lack of conviviality and camaraderie. Loneliness is out and togetherness is in. For, as any cottage owner can tell you, you seldom go to your cottage with just your own brood. Every child in the family decides he cannot abide even one weekend without his bosom buddy, so you never lack for extra company.

Among that happy group there is usually one little darling who can barely dog-paddle, but who decides to swim across the lake. You have the wonderful choice of sitting it out alongside in the rescue rowboat, or enjoying the tension of watching through binoculars from shore, waiting for the telltale signs of exhaustion which call for a speedy launch of the rescue craft.

Speaking of boats, the motors on these conveyances are the most finicky inventions of all time. They eat spark plugs at an alarming rate; and if the gas/oil ratio is off by so much as an eyelash, the motor konks out.

It is guaranteed to happen just when you are halfway across the lake with four old aunties whom you have taken out for a scenic spin. It can also be guaranteed when you are water-skiing, especially when the temperature hovers around sixty degrees and you don't feel like falling in the lake. And when it is at ninety-eight degrees and you are at the farthest point from land, a konk-out is inevitable, thus requiring you to paddle all the way back.

Another enjoyable aspect of owning a cottage is the number of people you get to feed. In fact, we have christened our hideaway the "McDonald's of the Northwoods." Sometimes it gets so busy at our place that I swear someone has put us on the map as an historical marker.

Of course it gets hectic at times. But I would never go as far as the neighbors who hung this sign on the cottage next to ours: "This cottage is Dad's dream, Mother's nightmare."

SO MUCH FOR SELF-SERVICE

Remember the good old days when you could drive into a gas station and the Texaco man would come out and ask, "Can I fill it up?"

And then he would wash all the windows, check the oil, offer you a key to the rest room, give you a free plastic spatula and two cards for the bingo game (with a chance at a trip for two to Hawaii), call the screaming baby in the car seat "adorable," salute, click his heels, and sing: "You can trust your car to the man who wears the star...."

Times have changed. And I can't graciously accept the change.

I'm not too mechanical, and I can't get the hang of the U-Pump—Serve-UR-Self gas stations.

In fact, I've had so many disasters with those pumps that I'm running out of new places to go where they don't recognize me.

The other day I drove up, filled the car, and then couldn't get the gas hose back into the pump thing. (I suppose there are names for all this stuff, but I'm not too technical, either.)

I tried and tried to fit it back. Finally I just laid it down on the ground and got into the car. I now know what it takes to get that gas station person out of his glass cage: just lay the hose on the ground and he comes out of there like a shot!

Another time I got the gas in okay and the pump put back, but I couldn't get the gas cap back on the car. I finally managed to force it on. Then when I put gas in the car the next time, I couldn't get the thing off. I had put the cap on upside down and the threads were forced and it all had to be fixed at the Ford dealership. At least, they got around to fixing it after they stopped laughing, which was quite a long time.

And the people who take my money at these U-Pumps are sure a far cry from the "man who wore the star." Most of them favor leather jackets and chew something. Maybe it's gum. They often have shifty eyes, too. I feel like they think I'm about to hold them up.

Actually, it's the other way around.

In fact, at the last station I went to, I cheerily paid the $5 for a snifter of gas without even a thank you from the person behind the money cage. I also had to pay him for the key to the rest room.

BYE-BYE BIC

Pens appear to be made of ordinary substance, but looks can be deceiving. They must contain a self-destruct mechanism, or at least have a built-in capacity for disappearing, in order to pull a vanishing act every time I look for one.

I can't tell you how many business letters I've written with an old eyebrow pencil, or how many grocery lists I've scribbled in lipstick because I couldn't find a pen.

Why do pens disappear? Is it some form of retribution for the time I inadvertently stabbed that girl with my Bic back in grammar school?

Just last week I bought a package of twelve ball point pens. You know the kind — the pens that are guaranteed to leak on your hands and your clothing for six months or until your entire wardrobe is stained with ink, but guaranteed also to write on paper for only three minutes before running dry.

I put them lovingly in a cup beside the telephone on the desk and stood back to admire the look of it. So organized. Twelve — count 'em — twelve pens all ready to write. No more scrawling messages in the dust on the end tables. No more letters to my mother written with green eye shadow. No more rummaging in the fireplace for a piece of charcoal so I could write an excuse to Junior's teacher. No more spelling out messages to the milkman with Scrabble letters. I had pens!

An hour later I looked at my cupful of pens and counted eight. Two hours after that there were five pens. By morning only one remained. I grabbed it. I fondled it. I wrote a letter to my mother-in-law with it. I laid it down for just a minute. (Even a fetishist has to take a break now and then.) And when I looked for it, it was gone!

I shrieked! I railed! I beat my chest! I bellowed! It was so unfair.

But I knew where those pens were. They had disappeared to that great desk in the sky along with the scissors, the vanishing Scotch tape, and the self-destructing paper clips.

LIFE IS A PICNIC—BUT WHO PLANS THE MENU?

Paying my weekly grocery bill has changed this normal-neurotic woman into an anxious weepy wreck.

The reason for this depressing change is simple. The whole gang is home now. All day. And that includes lunch.

I think if they didn't eat lunch, I would have enough money to take that cruise, join the country club, and have the TV fixed.

I knew it was going to be a long hot expensive summer when I was confronted by a teenage collegiate girl in my kitchen last week.

"We're all out of pop tarts," she shrieked.

"Who are you?" I asked.

"Your daughter, remember? I've been away at school. And we're not only out of pop tarts; there's not a cheese curl or an M&M to be found."

"I thought the last time we were together, you were on a diet."

"Mother! Honestly! That was last summer. I ate only yogurt the last semester of school and I'm actually underweight now. I can eat what I like."

"Oh, goody," I choked.

Another strange person accosted me. He looked vaguely familiar. Taller, of course, but he could pass for a blood relative.

"Mom, we're out of carrots, tofu, sprouts, endive, and pita bread," he declared.

Ah, I remember him now. The health food addict. He used to spit out his spinach when he was little.

Hildy wandered in. She's here most of the time. Too bad she's not one of ours. She's easy to please, eats only peanut butter and chocolate chips.

"Let me see," I muttered, "we need cheese curls, pop tarts, carrots...."

"Don't forget Cool Whip, Hershey's syrup, apples and popcorn," another voice chimed in.

"I'll get you the apples," I shouted, "but you can forget the rest. You don't burn off that many calories watching 'Wheel of Fortune.'"

I've just finished writing my congressman. I'm lobbying for a summer hot lunch program. ✓

A HEATED PROTEST

Dear Mother Nature,

I realize I wrote you last winter and begged for warm weather, but I fear you have gotten carried away.

Our countryside is now thawed out. Completely. You can turn down the heat and banish the muggies. Enough already.

"How hot is it?" you ask.

It is so hot the dog is scratching at the refrigerator door.

It is so hot my deodorant stick has melted.

It is so hot the kids aren't fighting. And if you know anything about kids, that's HOT!

It is so hot the cat is in the bird bath.

It is so hot I have to dry my hair before I can go out — and I didn't even wash it.

It is so hot the kids have turned on the sprinkler, but nobody has energy enough to run through it.

It is so hot that going to the dentist sounds like fun because his office is air-conditioned.

It is so hot that my husband says it is even too hot for — well, never mind what he says.

It is so hot that popsicles melt and fall off the stick after only one lick.

It is so hot no one is arguing about who used up all the hot water in the shower.

It is so hot I'm wondering if I could wear my muumuu to church, and if I did, would anyone notice?

It is so hot, Mother Nature—and believe me, I never thought I would admit this—that I miss winter. So, if you have a nice cool low-pressure system left over from the frozen days of January...well, could you send a little our way?

Thanks,

A Former Lover of Summer

PLAY DOH AND STEUBEN GLASS

Whenever I leaf through a copy of *Make Your House Beautiful,* I become so depressed about my surroundings that I decide I have two options: either sell the house and move, or tear it down and start over.

From reading that magazine, I've decided that the key to successful decorating is owning a chain of greenhouses. Have you ever noticed that in order to have a beautiful room you should have 173 Boston ferns in it? And at least half are suspended from the ceiling and not one is dripping water.

Once I tried hanging a Boston fern. I discovered that, if I watered it enough, it dripped for a day and a half. If I watered it less, it turned a nifty shade of brown before its fronds fell off.

The rooms for children pictured in these magazines have led me to believe the decorators have designed these rooms for a child of about twenty-seven years of age. My children's rooms are decorated in early Barbie doll and contemporary hamster.

As for the floor covering, if I ever get the junk cleared away, I'll let you know. But in these magazines, white shag carpeting is considered *de rigueur* for the toddler set, with a Raggedy Ann doll neatly propped in the corner. One room even had a beautiful live blooming mum plant.

The only live thing in my children's rooms, aside from the hamster, is an occasional frog.

Another criterion for a room with flair is an abundance of knick-knacks. Not the kind I have — the papier-mâché voodoo masks made in Cub Scouts, or the large Play-Doh sculpture inscribed "Happy Mother's Day," or the yarn wallhanging decorated with dried leaves and pine cones from summer camp. No, these houses sport porcelain birds, wicker elephants, and Steuben glass conch shells.

I can readily picture one of my children galloping through the house on a wicker elephant or listening in vain for the sound of the sea from a glass conch shell.

But the kitchen is always my favorite. It really gives me something to strive for. The only thing shown on the counter top is a wedge of brie cheese and a lime. Where, oh where, is the half-eaten bag of oreos, the sweet potato with toothpicks in the jelly glass, the remains of a peanut butter and jelly sandwich, the vase of dandelions, and the mason jar with the caterpillar in it? Where?

And the refrigerator not only lacks fingerprints, it doesn't even have one crayoned masterpiece hung on it.

I have decided not to move. I'd rather look at a Play-Doh sculpture than Steuben glass any day.

CAN A CLOSET BE HORIZONTAL?

I envy that woman on TV who has such a difficult job doing the family laundry because her children's clothes are covered with ground-in dirt and her husband soaks his overalls in motor oil. At least her gang's clothes *need* to be washed.

At our house most of the clothes that wind up in the hamper are clean. Now, I ask you, where's the challenge?

Just the other day I asked my daughter why she had twelve sweaters in the laundry hamper when the temperature had been ninety degrees for a week.

She replied, "I was trying them on to see if they still fit; and when I was finished, I put them all in the hamper."

The frightening aspect of this exchange is that it sounded logical to me at the time.

Another criterion for pitching clean clothes into the hamper is whether a sibling has worn another's clothing.

"Why is this jacket in the wash?" I screeched at one darling. "I just washed it yesterday."

"Because Lana borrowed it, that's why."

"That doesn't make it dirty," I snapped.

"Does too," Little Darling answered back. "It has Lana's germs all over it."

And towels. They seem to multiply. I grab up every towel in sight, throw them into the washer, and thirty minutes later when I walk past the bathroom there are fourteen towels scattered around. Obviously, they mated and begat while I wasn't looking.

And I would like to know what the kids have against hangers. My son carefully lays out his fast-food uniform — if it's clean — on the floor of his room. (If it's dirty, it joins the pile of sweat socks, shorts and jeans in the corner, in which bacteria are growing at a rate any biochemist would envy.)

Another daughter has layers of clothes on the floor of her room. Winter, fall, spring and summer ensembles are all spread about the room. I've often wondered what is on the bottom of the pile. Probably the dress she wore on the first day of kindergarten. She's a junior in high school now.

Recently I decided to confront them.

"See this triangular piece of wire with the hook on top? It's called a hanger. H-a-n-g-e-r. It hooks over the rod in your closet. You put clothes on the hanger and then hang it on the rod...."

Four pairs of eyes stared at the contraption. Finally one pair met my gaze, and their owner shook his head knowingly.

"Hanger, huh?" he said. "You know, Mom, it's a nifty invention, but it'll never catch on around here."

UP TO MY ELBOW

The last time I set up the ironing board, four children stared at it and then chorused, "What is it?"

That's a legitimate question around our house since the ironing board hadn't been set up since A.P.P. (After Permanent Press.) I consider the word 'iron' to be one of the uglier four-letter words.

Over the years I have learned to positively avoid any clothes labeled *"Touch up with cool iron"* or *"Some ironing may be desired."* Doing so has taken real ingenuity and creativity.

For example, I take wet clothes out of the washer and carefully lay them out on the kitchen counter. I find that by running my elbow and forearm over them — I use lots of pressure — the clothes come out almost wrinkle free.

"But, you told me to clean up my room."

And, thanks to this method, I now have one of the strongest forearms in our neighborhood.

But the latest trend back to natural fibers has not been a help to me. Actually, those two little words, *"All Cotton,"* have tempted me to take up my picket sign and strike.

Recently my teenage daughter brought home a blouse with those dreaded words on the label.

"Do you like it?" she asked.

"Sure, I like it. It looks like something you'd wear on a walking tour of Transylvania."

"Mother, have you no sense of style? It's a safari shirt and it's 100 percent natural fiber."

"You mean it has to be ironed?"

"Yes, but you've told me never to mention that word."

"Didn't it come in polyester?" I asked.

"A safari shirt in polyester!" she scoffed. "That would be like having a pair of jeans with an elastic waistband."

"I have a pair like that," I replied huffily. "So why can't they make safari shirts out of drip-dry material?"

"Maybe they did once upon a time, Mother, but I think that went the way of Fats Domino and the Kingston Trio. Out!"

"Well, my dear, if that's what you want, keep the shirt. But you will have to take care of it, feed it fabric softener, wash it by hand in cool water, and iron it."

The next day I saw my daughter with her safari shirt spread out on the kitchen counter. She was pressing it with her forearm.

Score one for heredity. ✿✿

I Need It, I Need It Not

Closets should be small. They should be just big enough for that one special outfit, a few pairs of slacks, and the "go with everything" blazer.

The trouble is, closets usually are big. After years of women complaining that every house should have big closets, architects and builders listened, and now most houses have big closets.

I have a walk-in closet which I share with my husband. He's neat. He wears only brown suits, brown shoes and brown socks. I'm sure that says something about his personality, but I'm not sure just what.

Anyway, because I have this huge closet, I can save everything.

Today I succumbed to the autumnal fever which grips me every year. It's a strange phenomenon which appears when the first leaves fall from the trees. It imbues me with a wild energy to do *it.* CLEAN THE CLOSET!

The top shelf is a wild jumble of sweaters. On the bottom of the pile is my high school sweater, a heavy wool knit the color of dried blood. I ask myself, "Who needs a high school sweater? Why am I saving this?"

I answer, "I am saving this because I might be invited to a 'fifties' party. Plus it is really warm. And if we turn the heat down any more, I just might be glad to have it."

The sweater goes back on the shelf.

I continue to ask myself questions and I continue to answer them.

"Will polyester jump suits come back in style?" "Could I use that mini dress for a tunic top?" "Whatever possessed me to buy hot pink stretch pants?" "Will the maxi-look be 'in' again during my lifetime?" "Could I possibly sew little alligators on all those shirts to give them a new look?"

I lie to myself, too.

"Surely the material in these flare leg hostess pajamas is too good to throw away." "Of course polyester jump suits will be back in style." "And pleated skirts are ALWAYS 'in.'"

So far, I have a pile of stuff for Goodwill. It's a small pile, made up of an old pair of tennis shoes and a sequined blouse.

As I retrieve the blouse and put it back in the closet, I remember what my mother always said: "It's such a great feeling to get the closets cleaned."

CASH, BUT NO CARRY

America's motto could be "Do It Yourself." We don't need help. We are the ingenious, independent, industrious, self-sufficient Yanks.

We are encouraged to do everything ourselves—lay our own floor tile, wallpaper every room with sticky squares, fix our own cars, pump our own gas, be our own psychiatrist, scrub our own carpets, build our own houses, be our own lawyer, and fix our own salads when we eat out.

Do it yourself is as American as baseball, motherhood, and apple pie.

The latest in our do-it-yourself society is the no-frills, bag-em-yourself warehouse grocery.

Remember the friendly butcher, the polite bag boy, the smiling produce manager? At the new Pack 'n Save store they're only fond memories.

Pack 'n Save is a cavernous warehouse with products, still in their open-top cartons, lining the aisles. It's a shrine of consumerism. Generic foodstuffs, the latest craze, are everywhere and case prices are displayed in the event that you really want to stock up.

It's every man for himself. After you guide your oversize cart up and down the aisles, trying to decide whether to buy generic, private label, or—throwing caution and the budget to the wind—actually buying brand names, you come to the check-out counter. Now it's hustle time.

Being a bag boy looks easy. Remember how he nonchalantly packs up the groceries and it all turns out neatly bagged with heavy things on the bottom. Well it's not as easy as it looks.

At Pack 'n Save *you* are the bag boy. As the food rolls quickly down the moving belt, you try not to throw too many canned goods on top of the bread.

After my first week of squashed bread and broken cookies, I tried putting all the canned goods in one bag. Great—until I had to lift it. I was willing, but my back had other ideas.

The doctor says I'll be fine in a few weeks. He prescribed complete abstinence from warehouse groceries for at least a month.

I hope this doesn't sound too un-American, but I was only too happy to oblige.

GOING GOURMET

For years my idea of gourmet cooking was adding parmesan cheese to the spaghetti sauce, and sometimes sprinkling bacon bits on the green beans. Or, on really special occasions, adding white wine to the cream of chicken soup before pouring it over the chicken.

I admit I never received any great compliments on my

cooking, and dinner party guests usually reserved their oh's and ah's for the after-dinner mints. But it was good plain fare, and no one ever got ptomaine from supping at my house.

All that changed recently when I flipped on the TV and came face-to-face with Julia Child who was peeling her broccoli. I was impressed. I don't even peel carrots; I tell the kids the skin is good for them. I watched, with fascination, as she prepared a "simple" dinner.

That evening I was greeted with the usual "What's for dinner?"

"First," I announced in regal tones, "we're going to start off with celery root dip and rice crackers."

Five pairs of eyes glazed over.

"Gee, Mom, we're sorry you're sick."

"I am not sick," I answered shrilly. "We are dining 'a la Child' tonight."

The celery root dip did not make a hit. Number One Son said it reminded him of coleslaw—gone bad. Our nine-year-old saved her portion to make a "plaster" village for her school project.

Undaunted, I served the crepes layered with ham and swimming in cheese sauce.

Dinner was quiet. Everybody was busy scraping the sauce off the ham and pouring maple syrup on the crepes, which they mistook for pancakes.

I cleared my throat and said bravely, "I hope you have all saved room in your tum-tums for dessert."

"That all depends on what it is," my husband answered diplomatically.

I waved my wire whisk grandly. "Chocolate bombe, you lucky gourmands."

The bombe bombed. Everyone felt cheated when they found out it was molded ice cream.

The next night I was greeted with the usual "What's for dinner?"

"Spaghetti," I answered, "with my famous parmesan sauce."

The cheers were deafening.

THE CULT OF CLIPPING

One thing common to most women is the fact that we cut out recipes.

I'm not sure why the sight of a recipe so stirs us to keep collecting, why another recipe for hamburger surprise so excites us.

Even if we already have four recipes for everything, even if we live alone and eat only yogurt, we continue to snip away.

I have a huge collection of recipes, all flung into my recipe drawer without rhyme or reason. If I'm looking for that recipe for zucchini cake, I have to sort through twenty years of clippings to find it.

Oh, I started off neatly enough. I had a little recipe box and all the recipes were on neat little cards. That lasted about a month. Then I started cramming the recipes into the box; and when I couldn't cram in any more, I shoved them into a small drawer. The collection outgrew that, so now they're in a big drawer, and that's full! I have visions of someday keeping my recipes in a room by themselves.

I tried to organize them during the big blizzard of '82. I took looseleaf folders and labeled them: Meat, Fish, Poultry, etc. My undoing was that I never had enough labels for miscellaneous items like pickled figs and mock Twinkies. So the whole drawer became Miscellaneous.

And I have never bothered to try out most of the recipes. I have high hopes as I flip through magazines and think, *Ah, crown roast of pork with fresh apple dumplings would make a great dinner.* But I'm always fresh out of crown roast of pork or apples, and then I find there's no such thing as instant dumpling mix. So another recipe gets lost in the drawer.

I think I know why I still clip recipes. It's become a habit like picking up after everybody or changing the sheets once a week.

One thing that's comforting about this habit is the thought that after I'm gone, if somebody goes through my recipe drawer, he will be bound to utter in reverent tones: *"This one must have been some cook!"*

✂✂✂

I WISH...

When college age children come home for summer vacation, it often releases a flood of memories of moments shared, opportunities missed.

When I see my six-foot son trying unsuccessfully to start the lawn mower, frowning at it and then giving it a small kick— just for a minute there I see him in his sand box at age three. He has the same look on his face now that he had then when his big sand castle collapsed.

When a daughter, just home from college, is struggling to wrap a wedding present for her friend, and her face shows such rapt concentration and her brow is furrowed as she tries to make a big perky bow—I'm back in time watching her struggle to tie her shoelaces into a perfect bow.

I wonder how many accomplishments of my children I missed because I was too busy doing something else.

If I had it to do over again, I wouldn't scrub the floor as often—but I would take more time for walks with them.

I wish I had said "no!" to more committee meetings and had answered more of their questions carefully. *("Is a string bean and a human being kind of the same, Mommy?")*

I wish I had dusted less and had built more snowmen with them.

I should have yelled less when their adventuresome natures made them experiment in the kitchen: as kindergartners cracking eggs on the floor to see if chickens really do come from eggs, or dumping their milk glasses upside down to see if milk pours out the same way it pours in. (Then again, maybe you do have to yell sometimes!)

I wish I had spent more time laughing with them and less time wishing they'd grow up.

I wish I had never shouted at my daughter, "You're acting like a two-year-old!" before remembering that she was just that— a two-year-old.

I wish we had smelled more flowers together, played more games, read more stories, talked together more often, and shared more peanut butter sandwiches under the tree in the back yard.

Sometime, while I was busy wishing they were big enough to walk or talk or dress themselves or go to school or stay home without a babysitter...they grew up.

§ § §

An Unwritten Law of Nature

Mothers are not supposed to get sick. Wives are not supposed to get sick. It is an unwritten law of nature. Children and husbands subscribe to this law.

I was sick recently. All eight (or is it twelve?) sinus cavities were filled to bursting. My eyes felt like they were full of ground glass, and my throat felt like I had swallowed a razor blade. If I could have located the thermometer in my generally weakened state, I'm sure it would have read "Take two aspirins and go to bed for a week."

My family noticed me slumped across the ironing-board.

"What's with her?" they chorused.

"I am sick, sick, sick," I croaked.

They looked bored.

"Does that mean you're not going to bake chocolate chip cookies today?" the youngest asked.

"It means I may die if I have to walk more than three feet," I answered.

"She sure does exaggerate, doesn't she?" exclaimed one of the teenagers.

"Yeah, when they get older they seem prone to hyperbole," another teen piped up.

I thoughtfully chewed my cough drop and wondered whatever possessed me to have children.

"Well, I've got my first football game today, Mom. You won't forget to come, will ya?"

"And I need a ride home from school today."

"And don't forget to pick up my suit at the cleaners."

I stared at them through gritty, watery eyes. Maybe I wasn't hearing them. Maybe I was delirious.

I thought about the cough medicine commercial on TV. The woman is in bed, surrounded with pillows, blankets, and facial tissue—all that good, comfy, curing stuff. Her husband brings her a cup of tea and a pill.

"Here's some baby aspirin, Mom. Now can you come outside and help me with my snowman?"

She says, "I wanted a coughing, sneezing, fever, aches, pains, sore throat, get-a-good-night's-sleep cold medicine. And you have the nerve to bring me tea and a cold tablet."

He is apologetic. Grabbing his coat (it's usually raining in this scenario), he says, "Honey, I'll go back to the store right now and get you the nighttime cough medicine."

I ask you, when is the last time you got that kind of treatment when you were sick?

Ah, well, I shouldn't complain. My son's football coach let me leave the game early. He said I looked so bad I was scaring his players.

WORRYING IS AN ART

Worrying is an art. I don't mean the common, now-and-then type of worrying about inflation, or your children's grades, or whether Nancy Reagan will have enough tablecloths to go around.

I'm talking about worrying as an avocation. A year-round day in and day out, every minute, full time kind of worrying. That's the type of worrier I am.

I'm the one who worries, all during a two-week vacation, whether I turned off the stove, even though a friend is checking the house daily during our absence and would certainly turn it off if I did forget.

I worry about fires in hotels, too. I even gave my husband a smoke alarm to carry on business trips, but he said it takes up too much room in his suitcase.

I worry about the car breaking down and leaving me stranded in sub-zero weather, even though I'm only making an eight block trip to the grocery store.

I worry about my eldest child who is away at college because she doesn't eat right and she works too hard and she's too trusting and what if she goes out with some creep and he kidnaps her and takes her to Death Valley and she doesn't have change to make a phone call.

I worry about my second eldest because he eats right and paces himself and is sensible and how long can this last? Ha! Not too much longer and then he'll change and he'll forget to be sensible and he'll drop out of college and join the Foreign Legion. What a waste!

And I worry about the third eldest because she's really got it all together and for a high school student is very mature and for a teenager she's extremely likeable. But just give her time. She'll probably be making plans to join a weird cult and sell flowers on the street corner and change her name to "Mirage" and never come home.

And I worry about the youngest. She's eleven. She is so talented and musical and you know what happens to talented musical people. Hollywood beckons and then it's the whole bad scene: crooked agents, failed marriages, the valley of the dolls.

So worrying, for me, is more than just a hobby; it's a full-time job. But then, as you can see, I've got a lot to worry about. ✔✔

THE WEIGH OUT

I regard having an annual check-up with about the same enthusiasm as having an impacted wisdom tooth extracted.

My terror is not assuaged one bit as I wait in the doctor's outer office. Have you noticed that the magazines in the waiting room don't offer much to take your mind off what is in store for you?

Last week as I waited I found I had two choices in reading material: a 1969 copy of *Popular Mechanics* or a well-read book of *Bible Stories for Children*. I opted for the former.

Actually, it wasn't a bad choice. I was just getting into an interesting article titled "The Right Wrench Can Make A Difference" when I heard my name called. I ignored it. Unfortunately, the nurse recognized me, and I had no choice but to follow her down the long hall to the examining room and the dreaded scale.

I have come up with myriad schemes to beat the weigh-in. I have feigned dizziness, saying stepping onto the scale would bring on the vapors. I have listed my height as six feet two inches, in the vain hope that no one would notice that I was five feet eight, and thus my weight would correspond favorably with my newfound height.

I have even been known to keep one foot on the floor, claiming my lopsided posture came from an old cheerleading accident.

The only fun weigh-in I ever experienced was the time the doctor misread the scale by thirty pounds and told me I was underweight.

This time I decided to forego the drama and bravely accept the trauma of the scale. I would simply pretend I was a thin person. Mind over matter, so to speak.

After the weigh-in, I undressed and wrapped myself in a breakaway sheet. I just love those paper sheets. As soon as you wrap one around yourself, it starts proving it is biodegradable. Little rips and tears appear in the most embarrassing places. It's a real challenge to stay modestly covered.

As I perch on the edge of the examining table, wondering if the doctor will arrive before the sheet disintegrates entirely, I read all the documents on the walls.

Doctors seem to have diplomas on the walls in every room. Do they have copies made, or do medical schools hand out four or five sets of certificates at a time?

Some of these credentials are a trifle ambiguous. For example, there are always one or two which state that the doctor has successfully served in Hawaii. Served as what? A headwaiter? A surfing instructor? A guide?

When I finally finish reading all the wall doctrines and I am about to begin counting the holes in my paper sheet, the nurse opens the door and tells me the doctor was just called out on an emergency. She wonders if I could come back on Thursday.

I tell her I will be happy to come back—but I'm bringing my own sheet. ✚✚

A VERY SPECIAL LADY

Usually at some time in our lives we reach a point when our mothers' eccentricities and idiosyncracies are suddenly recognized as being charming and lovable personality traits.

I know my own children haven't yet reached that point. To them, I am still hovering somewhere between "old-fashioned" and "weird." But I've reached the time in my life when I appreciate my mother, quirks and all.

Just the other day she called me, long distance, to tell me basketball players shouldn't be too tall. She thought there ought to be a law prohibiting them from playing the game if they are over six feet four inches tall. She doesn't think it is fair to the shorter players in the NBA to have to compete against players measuring seven feet.

Years ago I would have scoffed at this bit of creative reasoning. Not now.

I may still question her logic on occasion, but never her loyalty. I have often speculated that if I ever told her I had just committed murder, her only comment would be that I must have had a very good reason. Loyalty like that can only come from your mother.

Her timing is great, too. She's always around when I need her.

When I was little and had a nightmare, she came when I called.

When I was a tree in the school play, she sat proudly in the second row.

When I thought I knew everything, she was patient.

When I admitted my mistakes, she never said, "I told you so."

When I thought I couldn't possibly succeed, she always argued that I couldn't possibly fail.

When I complained about life in general and my life in particular, she listened.

When I was making those hurried middle-of-the-night trips to the hospital, about to give birth, and needed someone to stay with the older children, she came.

When I felt the fear and worry a mother feels for a very sick child, she comforted me.

Thanks, Mother, for your great sense of timing. And by the way, maybe basketball players shouldn't be too tall.

SIXTIES

At a party recently, I was a quiet onlooker as a group of people spent a considerable amount of time discussing the sixties. As they reminisced about their participation in rallies and protests, I grew even more withdrawn.

Why was I so quiet? Had I been too young to protest—

or too old? Neither. During the sixties I was married and immersed in child rearing.

While thousands of my peers were protesting the war in Vietnam, I was making formula and washing diapers.

As university buildings were taken over by groups of demonstrators, I bought baby food by the case.

While cities burned and activists marched, I faced the problems of toilet-training toddlers.

While students staged sit-ins, I discovered new and better ways to remove crayon drawings from wallpaper.

I spent the night of the 1968 Democratic convention having a riotous time. I was in the labor room, about to give birth to our fourth child.

When Dr. Benjamin Spock was arrested, it reminded me that my copy of his book on child care was three years overdue at the library.

Betty Friedan's book, *The Feminine Mystique,* and its premise that women do not feel needed, struck me as hilariously funny. I had never felt so 'needed' in my life.

By the time I had figured out what the Beatles' hit, *Lucy in the Sky with Diamonds,* really referred to, the famous foursome had split up.

"Flower children" and other members of the counter-culture rarely surfaced in the hallowed halls of nursery school. And the only times I raised two fingers, I was teaching someone to count, not giving a "peace" sign.

Miniskirts were rarely found in maternity shops. Ditto love beads. And it's almost impossible to wear vinyl boots when your ankles are swollen.

Obviously, I lived through the sixties unscathed by

even a touch of radicalism. However, it has occurred to me that my lack of involvement is shared by many others.

I am certainly not advocating a return to radicalism. But if there are some of you who, like me, missed out on all the marching and feel you would like to protest something, I think I have the answer.

Meet me in the grocery store. We can share a protest over the prices.

Flight Fright

It pains me to admit I am afraid of flying, after Erica Jong made a fortune by admitting it and I haven't made a cent.

But the truth is, I don't even like that old adage "flying high." Whenever I hear it, my palms get sweaty. And listening to a rendition of *Fly Me to the Moon* makes me rush for the dramamine.

Yes, I do have a teeny problem.

However, over the years I have gathered a few handy hints which help me cope when I must get on an airplane.

Immediately after boarding the plane, I check out the pilot. Is he praying aloud? Is he whistling the theme from *Airport?* Does he look like he is lost and can't find the cockpit? Does he have his cap on backward?

If I can answer "yes" to any of the above, I abandon the plane!

I then check out the stewardesses. Are any of them wearing parachutes? Have they donned their own oxygen masks? Are they passing around insurance policies? Are they removing their rings and other valuables and throwing them onto the tarmac?

If they are not engaged in any of these activities, it's safe to take my seat and buckle up.

Now I'm ready for take-off. At this point I usually hum *The Battle Hymn of the Republic.* Then I grab onto the armrests and scream!

Once in the air, I plug in the earphones. It drowns out the engine noise, and I try to pretend I'm on a Greyhound bus. But I don't let go of the armrests; I firmly believe that helps hold up the plane.

I look forward to landing like a kamikaze pilot looks forward to his first flight. Landing means the flight is nearly over — but then again, it could mean it's *all* over!

I ask the stewardess to pry my hands off the armrests and then I grab one of those "in-flight" magazines. You know the kind. They have cute articles like "How to Make Avocado Pie" and "What to Pack on Your Donkey for the Trip Down the Grand Canyon."

It doesn't matter what the content is. I use it solely to avoid watching the landing. I open the magazine and place it over my face, hooking a few pages over each ear to keep it from falling off. That way, no matter what kind of landing it is, I have a great view of avocados or donkeys.

Once we have landed, I remove the magazine from my face and saunter off the plane, looking confident. If the stewardess asks if I've enjoyed my flight, I try to avoid shrieking, "You've got to be kidding!"

I hope these little hints will be helpful to those who have to fly. If not, all the phobic flyers of the world could unite; then trains are bound to make a comeback.

A CURE FOR CARBURETOR ARREST

We are a two-car family. Last week we were a two-loan-car family. Both cars became extremely ill on the same day.

The first car bogged down in the middle of downtown. It was a case of carburetor arrest. Its motor was humming one minute and was dead the next. After a few brief attempts at resuscitation amid much horn honking, we had to abandon it and call Ye Olde Repair Service for a consultation.

In hushed tones, the mechanic decided the car would have to spend at least five days in sick bay.

No matter, we thought. Just take your time and get well. After all, we do have another car, right?

Wrong!

Just a few hours later I got into the family station wagon and zipped down to the post office. Actually, zipped is too strong a word for our wagon's pace. Lumbered would be more like it.

As I came to a stop sign, the brakes went out. Evidently that little red brake light on the dashboard wasn't kidding when it lit up as I backed out of the driveway. I had no brakes at all. I drove home, using the hand emergency brake. Until then I had thought the roller coaster at Great America gave the most harrowing ride in the world.

At least the brake light on the dash works, I consoled myself.

Ye Olde Repair Service promised us two loan cars. They were half right. They brought us two cars, but only one liked to take us for rides. The black one didn't like to leave the garage. (I call it "the black one" because I couldn't figure out the year or the make.)

The other loan car was obviously part of a hard sell. It was an '82 Mustang with four on the floor.

I took one look at it and said, "I'll keep it! Don't bother fixing our cars. If you keep our two cars and I throw in my grandmother's cultured pearls, maybe we can call it an even trade."

The mechanic didn't accept my offer, but I could tell he was pleased with my reaction. Pure envy is hard to disguise. I now know what "covet" means.

I had a great time with that loan car. I drove the Mustang and my husband got to drive "the black one."

The only trouble was that at the end of the week both our cars had made it through surgery and convalescence and were well enough to come home.

The mechanic finally managed to pry my hand off the Mustang's stick shift and shove me into my station wagon. But not before he whispered in my ear, "Don't worry, honey. Next time your wagon breaks down, I'll send over a T-Bird."

Now, those are words to live by!

A Short Life of Long Service

Appliances have a way of breaking down at the most inopportune times.

I've had a dishwasher die just as I was about to load it with dishes from a Thanksgiving dinner for thirty-two people. My vacuum cleaner once dripped black oil all over the carpeting just as the real estate agent rang the doorbell to show the house. My oven has expired just after I had the dough mixed for forty dozen cookies.

Last week was no exception. The washer conked out just as I had twenty loads of laundry sorted for the big back-to-school washing bonanza.

It not only conked out—it died a watery death. It gushed its way to obsolescence spewing water everywhere.

I didn't know whether to call the repairman or Rent-a-Boat. I opted for the repairman. When he arrived, I greeted him by name. (We're old friends. I've given him enough business that he can retire early.)

"Hi, Oscar. What's a mother to do? All I did was turn on the washer and the flood began."

Oscar happily sloshed his way around the washer.

"Well, um, as I recall...this washer is eleven years old."

"Eleven? Are you sure? It looks like new." (That's the trouble with washers and dryers; they always stay looking shiny and new long past their prime.)

"Yup. I remember putting this one in. Eleven years for a washer—that's like 127 years for a person. Or is that dogs? Anyway, the motor is shot."

"Can you fix it, Oscar?"

"Oh, sure. I can fix it."

"Great!" I playfully splashed through one of the large puddles.

"But it'll cost you almost as much as a new washer."

(Why do they always say that?)

"And, of course, your pumps ain't what they used to be."

"Oscar, don't get fresh."

"I meant the washer."

"Well, then, I suppose I'll have to get a new one. I'd like the same model and color."

"Sorry, we don't stock this color anymore."

"You don't stock pumpkin gold? I can't believe it."

"It's true. Times change. All the young couples want pale almond now."

After he left, I felt depressed. When you find the color of your washer has been discontinued, it makes you feel really old.

¶ ¶ ¶

SEPTEMBER

SEPTEMBER

Harbinger of fall.
She lies to you.
You are willing to greet her, make her welcome.
You trade in your shorts, sandals, and coppertone
for sweaters, new shoes, and corduroy.
She rewards you with 80 degree weather.

SEPTEMBER

She likes to whisper in your ear,
"Remember...remember...."

SEPTEMBER

Squeaky new saddle shoes that pinch your feet.
Number two pencils with points so sharp they always break as soon as you try to write with them.
A new lunch box which gives such a satisfying "click" when latched and unlatched.
Milk money inside a white handkerchief and pinned to your shirt.
The agony of not knowing which room to go to.
The ecstasy of finding a new friend.
The pain of scraped and bleeding knees as you misjudge the height of the jungle gym.

SEPTEMBER

Driving the car to school for the first time.
The happy knowledge that you have a date for Saturday night.
Perspiring in your first cashmere sweater.
Suffering aching arms from carrying around too many books because your locker won't open.
The acrid smell of formaldehyde permeating the biology lab as you try to hold your breath while dissecting a pickled frog.

HOOL
CHOWE

SEPTEMBER

Watching your own child board the school bus for the first time, not even looking back as you wave goodby and try (unsuccessfully) not to cry.
Filling out health forms and car-pool timetables.
Fighting end-of-summer lethargy.
Readjusting to the quiet stillness of a house filled with echoes of childish shouts and laughter.

You greet the start of another academic year.

SEPTEMBER

It's nice to have you back.

U-HAUL IT ALL

When college-age children return to school, they don't travel light.

I learned this the hard way when I overheard our son talking on the phone.

"Who was that?"

"Ace U-Haul," he answered. "I called to reserve a truck for the trip back to school."

"Ha, ha. That's funny," I chuckled. "Why do you need to rent a truck to haul a couple of suitcases and a stereo. We got your stuff down there in the car last year."

"That was last year. This year we're making one dorm room into a living room, and we'll all sleep in the other room."

"Oh." I quit chuckling. "What are you taking?"

"Not much, Mom. Just that old brown sofa in the basement, the two gold chairs that used to be in the family room, a floor lamp, and two table lamps. Oh, and could you spare the card table and chairs?"

"Actually, I don't think I can spare any of this. And how will all this fit into a dorm room?"

"Don't worry, Mom, it will fit."

"Sounds cozy. That room is at least nine feet by twelve feet. Maybe you can build an upstairs or suspend the sofa from the ceiling...."

"Nah, it'll be great. Now we still need a rug, end tables, and maybe a wet bar."

"Of course, I wouldn't want to see you roughing it. How about taking the pool table. Then the basement rec room would be completely bare."

"We thought of that, Mom, but we're striving for a certain ambience. The pool table wouldn't add anything. But some big orange floor cushions would. Do we have any?"

"Gee, the last time I checked we were kind of low on big orange floor cushions. Would you settle for a yellow bean bag chair with a small tear and no beans?"

"Mother, come on. This is going to be nice. A place to boogie and party."

Just then the phone rang. It was my daughter.

"Mom, I've got great news. I found an apartment so I won't have to be in the dorm this year. I thought maybe I could have the brown sofa, the old gold chairs, the...."

I cut her off. "You're just five minutes too late. Would you settle for a yellow bean bag chair and a pool table?"

DON'T FORGET THE TEDDY BEAR

For the first time in eighteen years one room of my house is pristine, neat, and spotlessly clean.

I owe it all to my oldest child. No, she didn't clean it. She moved out. She is now in college.

Gone is the blaring stereo, the litter of shoes by the bed, the profusion of green plants and half-finished cans of Tab. She took everything with her. The bed is still there, though. She tried to take it but it wouldn't fit in the U-Haul.

When a child goes away to college, she takes everything. It's as if she's never planning to return. A kind of rite of independence takes place. It seems to be carved in stone that, when one goes off to college, one must take all one owns, plus all the extras that will fit in the transporting vehicle.

"I can't wait to leave home, go to college and do my own thing."

This strange rite includes packing up all the winter sweaters, coats, parkas, skis and boots, even though it's ninety degrees and she plans to return home again in October.

This necessitates buying wicker hampers and baskets to take to school to store all the sweaters and coats and boots.

After she's packed and gone, I realize certain items are not around any more, like the small step stool from the kitchen, the family hair dryer, the curling iron, the novel I was reading, and all the throw pillows from the couch in the den. She had been eyeing the TV with relish, too, but I was able to stop her before she carted that off.

Somehow she managed to pack everything into a dorm room, leave space for a roommate, and still have room to walk sideways. This is remarkable, considering the fact that the roomie brought one of everything, too—plus a refrigerator, a TV, a bean bag chair, an extra dresser, and carpeting.

How they fit into that room is a miracle. I opened the door and just threw myself in the general direction of the bed. Navigating around all that stuff was too much for me.

I noticed one box contained her old teddy bear, the one Santa gave her on her first Christmas, the one with no eyes any more. His fur is worn down from fluffy to plushless.

I felt my eyes watering, and I swallowed hard.

"What's the matter, Mom," she asked.

"Hay fever," I answered. "Just hay fever." ✿ ✿

To My Eldest Child

Dearest,

You've probably checked the length of this letter and wondered what's gotten into me. Usually my letters to you are more like notes dashed off in a hurry, tucked into a box of chocolate chip cookies, and followed up with a phone call. It seems like life has a way of hurrying us along and letters seem too slow for our fast pace, so instead we "reach out and touch someone" by phone.

And that is really the point of this letter: time going by too quickly, and my wanting to snatch precious moments and hold them so they can be examined and savored, and even wishing certain moments of life had never happened at all.

Now that your own life is moving so fast and you have only a few weeks left to be a teenager, I want to reach out and capture some moments we can look at together—if you will let me.

Now you call a room in a dormitory "home"—and where your home used to be is "my parents' home." How quickly that changed.

You know, you were the one who gave us that title: PARENTS. We were not parents until you were born. You were the first child and I practiced being a parent on you. You're probably thinking that sounds terrible. And you're right. But at least it's honest. And it's not an easy thing to admit.

You are now almost the same age I was when I married. And when you were born ten months later, I had to learn parenting —fast! So, as the first-born, you were the guinea pig.

When you cried, I wasn't sure whether to pick you up or to let you cry. Would I spoil you by picking you up? If I let you cry, was it good exercise for your lungs? I wondered—and sometimes I let you cry and sometimes I didn't. My second, third, and fourth babies were a lot luckier. By then I knew that picking up and cuddling a crying baby is good for him and his mother.

When you started school, I was anxious. Would you measure up intellectually? Would you have friends? Would you perform well? Of course you did, but I didn't know then whether you would or would not.

As a result, you had to suffer my preoccupation with your schoolwork, your clothes, your hair. You heard a lot of "Stand up straight," "Don't wear the striped shirt and the flowered pants," and "Let Mother fix your hair." It was all done out of love and fear, but you couldn't have known that when you were six years old. All you knew was that sometimes it hurt your feelings.

And then came the big daddy of all fears, the time of giant trepidation: the teenage years! You were the first to have a boyfriend, go to parties, drive a car. And I was still practicing on you.

Oh, the mammoth rage I felt at your first lie... the horror I felt in me for your mistakes! All the ordinary teen-age problems were thrust upon me, and I lost my perspective and my patience. I was afraid I was not doing my job as a parent. I was anxious that you never make a mistake. So when you did make a mistake, even a small one, I came down hard on you. Too hard. And you must have felt confused and angry and hurt. I was still practicing.

When your brothers and sisters came to the same forks in the road, I was prepared. I had been through it all before. I had the battle scars and the guilt to prove it. I didn't have to practice any longer. I was more sure and confident. I knew more, then, about the perils of being a teenager. I also knew there isn't too much a parent can do except be there.

Now you are on your own. You talk of your own apartment next year, and of graduating from college and pursuing a career. there's no need for me to inflict any more inept parenting on you. And despite all my awkward efforts and all my blunders and all my practicing on you, you have grown into a beautiful person—someone I like as well as love, someone who is kind and generous and good.

I wish I could take time back and stop it and start all over. But of course I can't. It's too late for the two of us to undo some of those scenes, but maybe it's not too late to be of some help to you. Maybe, because I can say this to you now, it will help so that someday when you have a family, your first child will not be subjected to practice parenting. Then again, maybe every parent has to practice, to make his own mistakes. I hope not.

I do know it's never too late to apologize, and I'm grateful for that. I'm sorry for any pain I caused you, any hurt, and most of all I apologize for practicing so long.

I love you.

Mother

THE SILENCED SOUNDS OF SUMMER

School is back in session and mothers all around the country are hearing sounds they haven't heard for months.

They're hearing the phone ring, shattering the silence. What makes this special is finding the call is for them.

They're hearing the clock tick and the refrigerator click "on." They're hearing the soft thud as the newspaper hits the front porch. They are hearing a lot that they couldn't hear through the summer noise.

They're hearing nothing at all from the direction of the shower. There's no one in it for a change. And there's nothing to show for its past use except a nice growth of mildew along the shower door.

Mothers are seeing things they haven't seen in months, too. Like the gouge in the kitchen table, made by a screw driver as someone repaired a stereo speaker.

And the worn spot in the carpeting in front of the TV is noticeable now. Was it there all summer, hidden by the prone bodies of children?

Mothers are seeing the bedrooms left behind by college-bound children, now a little too neat after the lived-in look of summer.

A mother sees a tennis shoe under the coffee table and picks it up. And there's no one home to yell at for leaving it where it doesn't belong.

The quiet of the house, so still that a mother can now listen to her own thoughts, settles upon her. There are echoes around her. Snatches of voices drift in and out: "We're gonna go on a picnic." "I fell off my skateboard." "Gimme that!" "The balloons are for a water fight." "This plant will look nice in my dorm room." "Can I have the car?" "I picked you some flowers." Sounds of summer.

The echoes recede. It is quiet. The stillness becomes comfortable. It just takes a few days to adjust to it.

SPORTSPEAK

The poet, John Keats, described autumn as "the season of mists and mellow fruitfulness."

Around our house autumn is the season of first downs,

interceptions, fakes to the inside, and yards gained. Autumn is the season of football.

I wouldn't say I live in a house full of football fanatics. Fanaticism is too mild a term. Soon after we became engaged, I realized that football—to some—is more than just a game. It's a religious experience.

He changed our wedding date so the honeymoon would not conflict with the NFL play-offs. I should have sensed the power of the pigskin then but, sweet young thing that I was, I either couldn't grasp the implications or chose to ignore them.

I adapted rather well over the years. I crossed my legs and managed to wait and deliver our first child during half-time of the Packer/Colt game.

I learned never to pirouette naked in front of the TV screen, no matter what *The Total Woman* advised.

I learned Saturday and Sunday afternoons and Monday nights should be kept sacred for the resident football worshipper.

Then I found I had given birth to four football fanatics who could talk footballese before saying anything else. Other kids said "bye-bye." Our children's first words were "Tee-Dee" and "Offside."

So it's no wonder that, from September to January, footballese is the only language spoken in our house. For example, when my husband returned home from work recently, I asked him how his day had been.

"Not too bad," he answered. "Got off to a good start in the first quarter. Around half-time the day dragged a bit. But by the fourth quarter I could see no defenders

"Now, see, kid, it's third down and two, watch for a pass and pay attention to number 89 who could fake to the inside."

between me and the goal line. No overtime for me tonight. I just ran home to daylight."

"That's great, dear. What's the game plan for this evening?" I asked.

"I thought I'd go outside and, starting on my own one yard one line, I'd set up a sweep to the left. Then pass it to the wide receiver to go all the way."

"Oh, goody," I enthused. (He was going to rake the front lawn and Junior was going to help.)

Hannabelle arrived home from school. She picked up the newspaper, got a good snap from center, and sent it right into the ol' bread basket.

"Nice catch, Dad," cheered the gang.

"It was nothing," Dad yelled back. "I was ready for it. Great pass. Good blocking. Nothing to it."

I blew my whistle. "Time out," I said loudly. "What do you want for dinner?"

"Just the usual," they chorused. (Translated: hot dogs with mustard, in soggy buns wrapped in foil, with a side order of unshelled peanuts.)

"Okay," I answered. "But tonight I'm not going to put them in a box and hang it around my neck. You'll just have to eat at the table."

Ah, the season of mists and fruitfulness is upon me once again.

7 3 10

Who's on First?

Baseball is a clean sport. The players are constantly brushing dirt off their uniforms.

The language of baseball is clean and crisp too: "line drive," "high to the outside," "bases loaded," "pinch hitter," "relief pitcher." Players even bobble the ball, but never fumble. Precise language, easy to understand, characterizes baseball.

I like that.

On the other hand, football abounds in euphemisms: "The quarterback drops back, has to scramble, and finally lets one go to the wide receiver, who makes a diving catch for the first down." Translation: "The pass was complete."

By contrast, baseball seems a pristine, uncluttered sport without excess verbiage.

Baseball also brings back memories of my days as an outfielder. I was second string left fielder for the seventh grade Bluejays.

Our uniforms were blue denim pedal pushers, which cost $2.98 at the local Sears, worn with white cotton blouses with Peter Pan collars. As a traveling team, we played grade schools all over Orange County.

My best friend was second string right field. After school, we would change into our uniforms in the girls' restroom. Amid much giggling, we would pretend we were in our room at the Barbizon in New York City, dressing for a date at the Stork Club.

I wonder if professional players like Rollie or Reggie feel the same tension we felt when the second string was called in. I wonder if they could feel as nervous as I when the team got far enough ahead so that I got up to bat.

I prayed that I wouldn't strike out. The best hope was for a "walk." That would mean I had an eye for the ball, at least, and it would save me the humiliation of striking out.

I held the bat and trembled. The opposing team yelled, "Easy out! This one is shaking in her boots!"

The words stung me as I grasped the bat tighter. It was the bottom of the ninth and I squinted into the sunset and swung. A base hit! A single!

As I ran for the base, I thought no heaven could compare to being safe on first!

"Of course I love baseball," I tell my children now. "I used to play the game myself."

OOO

HALLOWEEN BEFORE HOLLY, PLEASE

Have you noticed that Christmas seems to be coming a little earlier every year? I used to complain that Christmas decorations were up in the stores right after Halloween, but now they're on display even before that holiday.

Last week, when I was shopping for napkins for my daughter's Halloween party, the only ones I could find had holly on them. So this week I thought I'd shop early for Thanksgiving.

"Where are your Thanksgiving decorations?" I asked the clerk.

She pointed to the half-price jumble table. "There might be something over there."

All I could find was a turkey-shaped candle with its wick broken off.

"This is all you have left?" I asked.

"Sorry, lady," she said. "You're pretty late asking for Thanksgiving stuff on the first of November. But I've got quite a few Christmas cards left. Why not have a look at them?"

"I still have Halloween pumpkins on the front porch," I grumped. "How can I buy Christmas cards?"

"Lady, if you don't buy your Christmas things now, you're not going to have any better luck than you did with Thanksgiving."

"But why do you have Christmas earlier every year?" I asked. "Who can be in the Christmas spirit in the middle of Indian summer?"

"Well, years ago when we put up Christmas decorations after Thanksgiving, it only gave us a month to sell. So we experimented and started a week earlier. Nobody seemed to mind, so the next year we moved it up another week. Now we start getting Christmas merchandise out on October fifteenth and it's great for sales. People have more time to buy...."

"You mean, in a few more years we'll be having Christmas on display in September?"

"Yeah, lady. I'd say you can bet on it."

I felt cheated out of the Christmas spirit. Santa shouldn't be smiling down on me when it's so warm I don't even need a coat. And Christmas cards shouldn't be for sale next to Halloween decorations.

The clerk interrupted my reverie. "Be sure and stop back soon. I expect our Easter cards to be in in a few weeks. Since you already blew Thanksgiving and Christmas, why not be here in plenty of time to shop for Easter?"

I assured her I would do that. "And Merry Easter to you," I shouted as I left.

FIRST SNOW

The first snow is magical. When you go to bed at night, the landscape is brown and barren. Leafless trees shiver in the breeze.

When you awake, the outside is washed white and new. There's a texture to the land again. Evergreen trees are laden with white, their branches heavy with snow. Bare deciduous trees are also frosted white and no longer look stark and lifeless.

What was your street is now a white lane, pristine and still untouched by tire tracks. The sidewalks have disappeared until some ambitious shovelers uncover them.

Children wake and run to the windows, their eyes wide with excitement, their noses pressed against the windowpanes.

"It snowed! Look at all the snow!" they shout.

Soon the backyard is full of footprints as they chase over the snow to build forts. The quality of snow is discussed as, like wise connoisseurs, they check the texture to see how packy it is.

If the snow passes the test, a project starts in the front yard—a snow man, a big one. He gains a carrot nose and charcoal eyes and your best scarf-and-hat set to keep him warm.

The first snow enchants and fascinates. Children hardly notice that their mittens are wet and their feet are almost numb from the snow that has fallen into their boots. Hats are lost and snowpants are soaked, but they don't seem to notice that, either.

But mothers do. It's hard to convince children that the snow will still be outside waiting for them after they come in to get warm and dry off.

Cross-country skis appear for brief forays around the back yard. Ice skates are finally located, to be slung over shoulders for the hike to the nearest outdoor rink.

Sure, it's a long winter, and shoveling is tiresome, and fuel bills are high, and even snow tires don't always keep a car from skidding. But all that is forgotten when the first snowfall comes. It's magic! ❄

LOVE AND THANKS GIVING

Thanksgiving is a good time to pause, slow our pace for a day, and count our blessings. It is a time when we are grateful for our friends and family.

I am reminded of two special friends whom we called Aunt Dorothy and Uncle John, even though we were not related. They were simple people. They never got their names in the paper or made a lot of money or did anything society would consider noteworthy.

Except for their love of music, there was nothing to set them apart. The only thing they loved more than music was each other.

Dorothy played the piano. She started playing when she was three, and had studied at Lawrence University in the twenties. Dorothy could make a piano do things most people can't make it do. If you heard her play, you felt a little richer, a little happier to be alive.

John played the drums. He and Dorothy did everything together for more than fifty years. They played in bands when they were younger. They played for schools and retirement homes as they got older. They were always busy making beautiful music together.

John loved his drums and he never stopped playing. Even after diabetes forced the amputation of both his legs, he still played the drums. Even after he was confined to a nursing home and his heart was weak and he was sometimes a little confused about things, he played his drums every week for his fellow nursing home patients.

Dorothy was always right beside him, accompanying him on the piano.

John died about two years ago. Dorothy still played the piano. But after John died, the times when she was able to play grew less and less frequent. With John gone, the light had gone out of her life.

Dorothy spent most of her last nine months in the hospital. She would be home for a time and then back in the hospital again. Last week we sent her a card, but she never received it. Dorothy died the day we mailed it.

I have a feeling that she and John are making beautiful music together again.

Sew What?

Last night, just before bedtime, my youngest child announced that she was going to be a chicken in the class play, and could I hatch her a costume by morning?

Not an easy feat, even if you sew and own a sewing machine. Oh, I used to have a sewing machine until my husband sold it to save money. He said I was ruining the budget by buying material which then went into clothes no one could possibly wear. A gross exaggeration!

It is true I did turn out a few outfits of questionable taste and wearability. For example, there was the dress I made for myself which had bodice darts placed so high it looked like I had twin tumors on my collarbone. And there was the coat I made for one of the children that had to be worn for a beach robe. And a pair of shorts (I didn't bother with a pattern) which had no zipper or buttons. The "Houdini Special," I called them, because there was no visible way to get in or out of them.

Still, there were some successful creations, too. I made a beautiful tablecloth. Of course, it originally was intended to be drapes for the living room, but everyone's entitled to make one mistake, right?

And there was the maternity sundress which was absolutely stunning. It was just a shame I wasn't pregnant at the time.

I do miss my sewing machine because I have difficulty sewing by hand. The other day, after I finished hemming a skirt, I stood up and discovered I had sewn the skirt in my hand to the one on my body.

I also have a problem with knots in my thread. I don't know what I'm doing wrong, but each time I push the needle through the material, it comes up on the other side with a big bunchy knot of thread. I've found that shrieking "Why me?" doesn't help.

The only timc the thread doesn't knot is when I have completed a project and attempt to tie a knot to finish it off.

Not only do I lack dexterity with the needle, but I'm not too well equipped with sewing materials. My sewing

"Mom, I'm gonna be in the school play. Do you think you can make me into a chicken by tomorrow morning?"

box contains two needles, seventeen spools of thread all tangled together, one useable spool of thread purple in color, and a package of snaps purchased in a fit of domesticity and never used.

One of the needles is a huge darning needle my mother gave me when I was a newly-wed with the hope that I would use it for darning socks. It is still in its original wrapping. The other needle has an eye so small that I suffer from severe eyestrain for a week after I attempt to thread it.

Obviously, it is not easy for a person like me to sew anything, much less a chicken costume. However, as I wield my teeny needle threaded with purple thread, I think things could be a lot worse. At least a chicken costume won't require any darts.

COPING WITH A CAST

Not long ago my husband and I went away on one of those "Break Away" weekends. The only trouble was that I took it too literally. I broke my leg.

After the first hazy days of pain had passed, it occurred to me that, while we are deluged with a plethora of self-help books, no one has yet written anything on coping with a cast. I can rectify that by sharing what I have learned, so that the next person with a broken leg will not have to cast about *(sorry!)* for information as I did.

One thing I found invaluable was a neatly lettered placard hung about my neck: "Yes, it's broken." "Yes, I did it skiing." "No, your laughing doesn't bother me at all." This saved strain on both my voice and my disposition.

Refuse the "Klutz of the Year" Award. Believe me, it's not worth the bother, and the trophy is hopelessly tacky.

Crutches should be used only in case of emergency. They were obviously invented by an Olympic track star with a gold medal in the hopping event. Rent a wheelchair or a walker.

I have learned that a break can really bring people closer together. Since my husband has to do the laundry, we have spent several romantic evenings discussing the merits of fabric softener and just what clothes should go into the dryer on the permanent press cycle.

Children can help too. So far, mine have learned to cook frozen pizza and to turn on the microwave oven. I should not have told my eight-year-old, "If you want chocolate chip cookies, you'll have to make them yourself." I don't think we will ever get all the flour out of the toaster, or remove all the chocolate chips that are embedded in the motor of the electric mixer.

Trying to dress while wearing a cast is not easy. Obviously, pantyhose are out and slacks are in. I did make one important discovery. The best way to pull slacks on over a cast is to use the barbecue tongs.

I discovered there are thousands of little chores that can be done sitting down, such as cleaning out my jewelry box and the junk drawer in the kitchen.

I also sent in for six get-acquainted offers from book clubs. I had a great time licking the little book title stamps and putting them in the little squares on the order blanks. Most of them promise six books for a dime. I picked all the books that carried the warning: "Absolutely shocking—not for the more sensitive reader!" It made me feel wicked...but use your own discretion here.

Via television I learned more than I care to know. I learned I have flabby hair. Cellulite can strike even thin people. Drano causes earthquakes. Ring-around-the-collar has reached epidemic proportions. Static cling can be grounds for divorce. If you are not serving stuffing instead of potatoes, you have not come a long way, Baby.

Watching television also made me realize I have had more than my share of good in this world. Somehow my husband has always received his raise, albeit I have never served Jell-O when the boss came for dinner. Friends still accept my dinner invitations, although my glasses may have water spots and my dinner plates can't be used as mirrors. My coffee is drinkable, even though Mrs. Olsen has never helped me make it. And I have never been forced to leave a grocery store for squeezing toilet paper. Yes, I am a very fortunate lady.

Be that as it may, I still suffered damage to my psyche as a direct result of breaking my leg. I developed a foot fetish. Whenever friends came to visit, I found myself looking lasciviously at their feet.

They all had two feet on the floor. They did not have to hop. They just put one foot in front of another. I found myself identifying people by their footwear.

My husband would ask if I had had any visitors, and I would reply, "Yes, one pair of high fashion boots dropped in but couldn't stay long. A pair of loafers and a pair of platforms brought over some cookies."

My doctor assures me this is a temporary condition. The fetish should disappear with the removal of the cast.

I believe I have succeeded in coping with my cast. If you find yourself in this same position, remember it could be worse. Be happy you're not a horse!"

CHRISTMAS RESOLUTIONS

The Christmas season is a great time for people who are organized. But for people like me, who don't get into the Christmas spirit until 11:00 p.m. Christmas Eve, the holiday is hectic.

Last year my fruitcake aged for twelve minutes. And I was so late mailing out my greeting cards, I had to cross out "Merry Christmas" and just leave "Happy New Year."

Ever since my children compared notes with the neighbor kids and found that oreos are not a traditional

Christmas cookie, I have made an effort to bake goodies.

I have a friend whose cookies are a work of art. Each one is perfect, decorated with precision—little ginger men, little Santas, little pecan fingers.

Somehow my pecan fingers look like the whole hand. And my cutout cookies are always in the shape of a bunny. For years my kids thought Santa was a bunny because that was the only cookie cutter I could find when I got around to baking for the holidays.

Some people handle shopping better than others. They have lists and sally forth with great aplomb. You can easily spot these people. They hum, usually softly, as they check out of the stores. Discreet snatches of *Joy to the World* or *God Rest Ye Merry, Gentlemen* pass from their smiling lips. They are confident, poised.

Then there are the others, like me. I don't hum. I lose my list. I get hung up on details. I'll spend two hours picking out Christmas wrapping paper and ribbon, only to discover I have not yet bought the presents to wrap.

I also have the problem of shopping for a husband who doesn't want what I think he should want for Christmas.

Every year he says all he wants is brown socks. It's not that he's such an altruist that gift-getting doesn't appeal to him. It's more a case of his not trusting my judgment or taste.

I've tried to get him something a little flamboyant. One Christmas I bought him a red bathrobe, but he said it was too racy. Another year I bought him brown socks with a slight pattern in them. He said they were gauche. I'll spend hours just trying to think of something to buy him, and when I do get an idea, I find it doesn't come in brown.

I'm convinced that anyone who is humming while shopping does not have a husband who wants only brown socks for Christmas.

This year is going to be different. I vow I will be organized. Never again will I wrap presents in aluminum foil because I ran out of wrapping paper. Never again will I finish putting up Christmas decorations in time for Valentine's Day. Never again will I get only to the M's on my Christmas card list. Never again will I be shopping at an all-night drugstore on Christmas Eve, trying to find the "perfect" gifts for all my in-laws.

Now, if someone will just hand me the bunny-shaped cookie cutter, I'll get started.

Customs and Candy Canes

Decorating the Christmas tree is part of the wonder and joy of Christmas to me. Aside from the beauty of the tree itself, it is the fun of rediscovering the ornaments every year.

At our house, the ornament for the top of the tree is special. We bought it on our first Christmas after we were married. It's a big, gaudy silver ornament made of thick plastic with a bell on each side and angel hair stuck around the bells. Hardly an heirloom. The price tag is still on the box — 89 cents. When we dashed out to buy it on Christmas Eve, it was the only one left, and we said we would replace it the next year with something prettier. We never did. Now we all agree it has a certain charm.

There's a box of unbreakable ornaments which I bought the year our youngest child was a baby. We hung them on the lower branches because her three older siblings delighted in putting her under the tree and pretending she was Baby Jesus.

There are big clumsy candy canes made out of rolled up paper with red crayoned stripes, made by one of the children in kindergarten. Every year the children ask why I'm putting them on the tree again. I don't answer. The lump in my throat makes it too hard.

There are little toothpick mangers made by chubby little hands in Brownies and Cub Scouts. And a paper Santa Claus with string run through so he moves like a marionette. There are styrofoam balls with sequins kept on with straight pins. Some have bare spots where the ornament maker got tired of sticking the sequins so close together and tried to hurry the job.

There are a few gold balls with the gilt chipped off. These are from my grandmother. She didn't have any fancy ornaments that I can remember, and these are all that remain from a box she gave me when I left home in California for married life in Wisconsin. Every time we hang these I have to tell the story of Grandma coming to

California in a covered wagon:

> One day on the journey, the wagons were drawn up in a circle and the women and children were left alone while the men went off in search of animals for food. Indians came. One Indian plucked Grandma's baby brother up in his arms. Great-Grandma traded the Indian a smoked ham in return for her baby.

And after all the familiar stories are told and the tree is decorated and the lights lit and the magic of Christmas makes us all children for a little while, we look at all the ornaments and each pick out a favorite. Everyone laughs when it is my turn to choose. I always pick the candy canes.

GRANDMA

The sun beat down on the glass doors of the patio, threatening to melt the fake snow right off the flocked Christmas tree. The children were dressed in shorts and playing with their new toys. It was Christmas Day, 1968, and it was hot.

I was hot too, wrestling with a big turkey which seemed thawed out but would not relinquish its plastic bag of innards. As I dug around inside it with my hand, it seemed I was engaged in some macabre birthing ritual.

At last, with a mighty whoosh, the giblets popped out and the stuffing could commence.

I brushed the perspiration from my forehead and wondered if this move to California was such a great idea. Imagine my voicing such doubts! I was a second generation Californian! Could I possibly be missing the Wisconsin winter? I pushed this thought out of my mind as the doorbell rang.

Mom, Dad, Aunt Janet and Grandma all crowded into the kitchen.

Grandma was eighty-four years old. She had come from Missouri to California in a covered wagon eighty-two years before. She had lost her only child, my father, many years earlier when I was only seven. Eleven years ago her husband, my grandfather, had died. She was alone, but never lonely.

Grandma was fun. She always had a story to tell, a laugh to share. Teenagers expecially seemed to seek her out. She still read the *Los Angeles Times* cover to cover every day. The facts of her life seemed so sad, but somehow no one had convinced Grandma of that. To her, just being alive was reason enough to be happy.

I pushed everyone out of the kitchen. *I would handle this,* I thought. My first big California Christmas dinner would be in my capable hands.

Grandma called after me, "Need any help, Dear?"

No, I didn't. Of course I didn't.

I started poking stuffing into the turkey. Then I expertly sutured up the bird.

I stepped into the living room where Grandma sat in the big rocker, thumbing through the pages of a magazine. Her hearing was poor and she hadn't heard me come in. She sat alone. Apparently everyone else had left on a tour of the neighborhood.

I remembered all those turkey dinners Grandma had fixed. I went back into the kitchen and removed all the sutures from the turkey. Then I rethreaded the big darning needle with coarse twine and called to Grandma to come into the kitchen.

"I'm sorry to bother you, Grandma, but this darned bird isn't cooperating. Could you give me a hand? I can't seem to sew it up."

Grandma laughed. "Heavens, child, of course. Just give that to me and I'll have it ready for you in no time."

She was smiling and humming to herself as she trussed up the bird. When she was finished, I thanked her. She beamed.

"I guess you still need your Grandma for some things."

I hugged her tightly. "I surely do," I said. "I will always need you."

It was our last Christmas in California. We moved back to Wisconsin.

It was Grandma's last Christmas.

ENOUGH TO LOVE A LIFETIME

Before I married and had children, I fantasized that I would be a mother like Jane Wyatt on "Father Knows Best." I would swish around in my full-skirted taffeta dress with the Peter-Pan collar, entertain effortlessly, and have two darling little children—possibly twins—who cooed and played and were always adorable.

It never crossed my mind that those adorable babies would spit up, get diaper rash, and grow into toddlers who would throw all the silverware down the furnace vents and throw their shoes out the car windows. Or that these same children would eventually become teenagers and accuse me of senility because I forgot to wash their gym clothes.

The husband in my fantasy was a charming and sophisticated bon vivant, someone who loved to dance and make wise and witty conversation. Somehow I never imagined that the man of my dreams would spend entire weekends sitting in his favorite chair in front of the TV watching any sport played with a ball...or that his witty conversation would consist of "Did you see that last play?" and "Do we have any popcorn?" (Note the royal "we.")

I had no idea I would develop midriff bulge at the age of twenty-four, that stretch marks don't go away, or that teenagers can make you deaf. Or that after teaching four children to print their names, I would have trouble remembering my own. Or that the nervous tic in my eye, which started when the eldest acquired a driver's license, will probably be a part of me until the youngest moves out.

Oh, I still have my fantasies. It's just that they are different now. I now dream of a perfect day when everything is canceled, and I won't have to carpool anywhere, and everyone likes what I have fixed for dinner, and I win the bingo game at the supermarket.

And if I've learned anything from being a wife and mother, it's to savor the good parts and laugh at the rest.

Comments about TOMORROW IS A RIVER

"...a good book...an incredible story..."

—Daniel Lusk in "Off the Wall"
National Public Radio

"...the book is an admirable accomplishment..."

—Jeremy C. Shea
St. Louis Post-Dispatch

"...a book above and beyond the ordinary... thoroughly authentic. Makes one feel every word."

—Brooks Sledge
Bookworld

"...worth reading and reading again. It deserves to become a classic."

—Peshtigo Times